T0147493

Family Stew
Our Relationship Legacy

ANNE SALTER, LCSW

iUniverse, Inc.
Bloomington

Family Stew
Our Relationship Legacy

iUniverse books may be ordered through booksellers or by contacting:

iUniverse
1663 Liberty Drive
Bloomington, IN 47403
www.iuniverse.com
1-800-Authors (1-800-288-4677)

ISBN: 978-1-4759-5481-4 (sc)
ISBN: 978-1-4759-5482-1 (hc)
ISBN: 978-1-4759-5483-8 (e)

Library of Congress Control Number: 2012918602

Printed in the United States of America

iUniverse rev. date: 10/10/2012

CONTENTS

AUTHOR'S NOTE

In the 1960s, I was a young girl in my early twenties and was following a lifelong dream of making my way in New York City. This was quite a leap for a small-town country girl. However, one of my adapted defenses was that I didn't let myself feel fear, so all I knew was the excitement of this longed-for change. Little did I realize that I already was in the throes of alcoholism, had incorporated my family's dysfunctions, and this would greatly hinder my ambitions. However, despite some very risky episodes while drunk, (I was a periodic binge drinker), I managed to complete a large part of my undergraduate degree at New York University and establish a career in retailing at a major department store. Best of all, I learned more about people of different backgrounds — racial, ethnic, and religious. I loved New York, but my dysfunction created much shame and disillusionment, not only with my ambitions to be a playwright, but also with my self-esteem. I left New York for a "geographic change" and married just six months later. In less than four years, I had four children, including a set of twins. I was not emotionally stable, nor in recovery, and not skilled to be a mother. Naturally, I chose a mate who was equally dysfunctional, and together we handed our dysfunction, and that of our muli-generational families of origin, to our children.

I participated over the years in many therapies. Finally in the early '70s, I came to a therapy group where the leader was doing "experiential therapy," including family-of-origin work. That was when I began to heal emotionally, to see myself more clearly, to heal my self-esteem. From there, I went back to finish my degrees and begin training in family-of-origin work, to establish my own practice using methods that I knew really work to heal one's Self.

Maureen Dowd, a Washington columnist, recently wrote: "Obama is the head of the dysfunctional family of America —- a rational man running a most irrational nation, a high-minded man in a low-minded age." She also quoted the Scottish historian Charles Mackay: "Men, it has been well said, think in herds; it will be seen that they go mad in herds, while they only recover their senses slowly, one by one."

We have to heal emotionally, ONE BY ONE, and that means looking into the "Family Stew" from whence we each came. This book is a product of my life's work, hoping to reach many people and to begin a real healing process, for ourselves and for our world.

— Anne Salter
December 22, 2010

DEDICATION

This book is dedicated to my children: Cristen, John, Richie, and Marc with all my love. My greatest wish has been to help them heal from our own "Family Stew." I am very proud of how they have all been persistent on a recovery path and continue to do healing work.

FOREWORD

This may be Anne's first book, but this book is the culmination of her life work. Today, at seventy, Anne has spent the second half of her life as a family-of-origin and addictions specialist. She is/has been dedicated to helping others understand and heal Self. I am honored to be Anne's friend and to have helped her begin the editing process. Anne and I know about pain; it first was inflicted upon us by our dysfunctional families of origin, and the continuous pain we inflict upon ourselves by the NOT KNOWING.

It is the NOT KNOWING that this book sheds light on. Read this book, and I can assure you that the understanding of Self resides within its pages.

Until you actually realize that there is such a thing as familial dysfunction in your life, you cannot be expected to deal with it. And then, by the time that you realize that your problems are a result of your negative childhood relationships and experiences, you often feel so screwed up and in pain, that you have no idea how to recover your Self. By this time, you may be medicating your pain by drinking, using drugs, over-eating, over-working, shopping, gambling, sexually malfunctioning, on your fourth or fifth marriage, or have children that are out of control and doing these things! But, you still have no idea why any of this happened or how you even got there! I promise that you will, after reading Anne's book.

When I met Anne, I was writing a musical about recovery called, Tough Love —The Musical. When I found out that she was a psychotherapist specializing in addiction disorders, I asked her if she would consult with me regarding addiction and recovery. I wanted to ensure my musical didn't insult anyone. I wanted my musical to ring true.

During Anne's consulting on my musical, I found out about her manuscript. I learned that Anne had stopped writing when she became ill a few years back. The more Anne spoke about recovery and her life's work, the more I knew her book needed to take the front seat to my musical. I offered to help her do the first editing of her book. It was my gift to Anne. Today, however, I believe I'm the one who received the true gift.

While working with Anne on Family Stew, I learned more about my Self, my Wounded Child, and my Inner Child than I ever have learned from reading any other book. Anne's book simplifies a seemingly complicated subject: Self. It has helped me tremendously to grow as a human being, as a woman, a wife, a mother, a daughter, a friend, and an aspiring author and playwright.

Foreword by Deni Boehm Sher

INTRODUCTION

We all have a personal story about our life, which incorporates chapters that are really stories within our story. One or perhaps several of these stories will reveal roots of traumas or life-changing events that have had a major impact on how we define ourselves, and therefore how these traumas or events have impacted our relationships. Most of these events will have happened when we were young, often in childhood. It almost always will involve something that occurred in a relationship.

The purpose of this book is to present a full etiology of the relationship with our individual Self, as it first develops in family relationships, then proceeds from this into all patterns of animate relationships and inanimate, and to help the reader reconstruct his/her story. It will include not only chapters on forming relationships with other people, our Self and our sexuality, but also on forming relationships with inanimate things, such as money, home, work, and religion/spirituality. Also, this new addition adds a chapter on our Relationship with Government and Politics, a major factor in our lives today. I always will refer back to the relationship with Self, which has been formed in the "family stew pot."

The goal is that this will be clear enough and the scope of possibilities wide enough, that it can serve as a guide and a tool to help the reader learn how to reclaim a healthy relationship with his/her individual Self and with all of his/her relating in the world.

My book is meant to take the reader to another dimension that is available for self-awareness beyond the scope of traditional, self-help books. It also will help to identify dysfunctional behaviors, beliefs, and patterns of functioning as symptoms of unresolved wounds from early relationship history.

"Study the past if you would divine the future." Confucius said. In terms of this book, that means you need to first study your past family history — especially family of origin — if you would like to understand and gain true awareness of the Self and its relationship composition, and what is predictable for you in the future of functioning in relationships. It is clear that we do not pay attention to the lessons of history, and then change our path in government. The process today begins to look like a theme of verbal civil war! In a new chapter in this edition I will address this in terms of our very dysfunctional family relationships in our government, primarily in today's congress.

I view the individual Self as similar to the meat, or main ingredient in a stew. As happens with the meat in a stew, it absorbs many flavors as it takes on bits and pieces of the other ingredients. As an individual child is formed in the womb and then birthed into a particular "family stew pot," it constantly is absorbing the flavors of the family members and how they relate to it and to each other. These relationship ingredients seep into the very being of the child as it grows and forms its individual Self. Even more flavoring ingredients, will be added in the larger stew pot of one's relationship experiences, particularly in early life. This is especially significant with teachers and other mentors of major influence. Sometimes, too, besides being flavored by ancestry, it is directly flavored by family of origin's family of origin, by grandparents. All of this flavoring becomes the core of one's relationship with Self. From this comes the driving force of one's relationships.

Today, there is widespread interest among people to find their roots." This includes genealogical research on the Internet and in libraries, visits to relatives, looking at family religious and cultural background (an extremely important element), and often widespread travel here and abroad. This is an important EXTERNAL search to find answers to such questions as: Where did my family originate? What did my ancestors experience and believe? How did they behave? Where do I come from?

This book, however, is about researching INTERNALLY into one's past relationships to better understand the beliefs, fears, unresolved conflicts, and any other confused feelings that reside inside Self. It is especially designed to help one discover what drives dysfunctional behaviors and choices in relationships with people, places, and things. For best results, I hope the reader will include an external ancestral search of the history and relationship patterns within his/her own family.

In taking my book to another dimension, a more comprehensive view, the reader can begin to address what may be stored in old, emotional, relationship wounds, which are creating dysfunctional behaviors. This is not only about seeing behaviors in relationships with people in a new light, but also (as I defined earlier) about a new way of seeing one's beliefs and actions in relationship with everything in life. Included in this book are many stories of people and how their adult relationship choices directly reflect their childhood "family stew pot." It is much like uncovering the source of an infection to treat it effectively.

The problem with just telling people to "get real" is that even though we may know that in some ways we don't feel or behave "real" (or are not true to Self), most of us who grew up in dysfunctional families and formed an Adaptive Self (which will be defined in Chapter 2: Family of Origin), do not know when or why we are not being real. We believe our Adaptive Self is our Real Self.

Books have only limited ability to access us below the neck, where many of our emotional memories and truths actually lie. And, even when access can happen, we cannot know how to handle it, process it, or change it by ourselves alone. My clients (who are also some of my mentors for this book), often comment about having read the many available self-help books and how they still remain stuck in dysfunctional patterns of living. I will emphasize and give guidance about seeking professional help, as an adjunct to what can be gained using what is offered here. If the reader wishes to get the most benefit from this book, he/she will find that including a trained, family-of-origin psychotherapist is immensely helpful.

Family Stew will clarify how we are trapped somewhere in the core of our relationship with our Self, protected by layers of wounds and defenses, and especially by lack of trust. Thus, we only know what we are aware of knowing.

In summary, this book will be a comprehensive exploration of relationship, as the core of everything we experience and for which we strive. The reader can begin to learn how to pursue a reconnection with the Real Self, wherein lies the core of relationship. By beginning to realize, learn, and understand one's dysfunctional, personal, behavioral themes, and road blocks (defenses), one can then discover what is required to change, in all areas of relationship, to have a more fulfilling life.

There are questionnaires throughout this book, meant to help you, the reader, to identify symptoms of stored wounds, and areas where you feel stuck when trying to make relationships work.

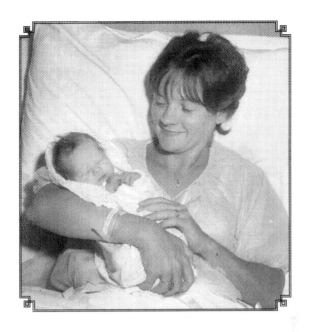

CHAPTER ONE

RELATIONSHIP AT BIRTH AND DURING INFANCY

The Shaping Begins

In the field of psychology, there is a belief that we are all born into this world as pure and unique beings. This belief is totally at odds with what is taught in some religions, which teach that we are born in sin. In those cases, we are given a shame message from birth, which, of course, immediately impacts one's relationship with Self. I will say more about this in Chapter 8 on Relationship with Religion.

I agree with the psychology version. I envision a newborn as almost a pure piece of putty to be molded. I say almost, because

---

there is a personality predisposition, a style of one's own, the Authentic Self, which will be played upon and affected by many, many external relationships. Out of these interactions with our unique Self and our environmental relationships will evolve a unique version of a human being: you.

We are not in the stew yet, but there already are impacts from the mother, who is part of the family stew into which the child will be born. Before the child is born, he/she is in the most intimate relationship there will ever be with another human being — literally attached to and totally dependent on the mother. I believe this is why more people have unresolved issues with their mothers than with any other relationship. This relationship has been so very close and intimate from inception, with our Self physically and literally torn or separated from her body at birth. My experience has been that people want mother connection/approval regardless of how dysfunctional and abusive she may have been. There often have been jokes about someone being dependent and wanting to go back to the womb. I believe that in many ways this is not a joke, because most of us never feel that secure again, that nurtured, or that peaceful. Thus, it is not so strange that it would have an appeal, especially if we do not experience enough nurture and self-affirmations as we grow and move on in life, and even more so if we had a negative experience in infancy. In this case, we may be stuck negatively or dependently enmeshed with our mothers. As a result, we might be prone to negatively enmesh in all important relationships. Based in the fear of losing closeness/intimacy, we create a kind of suffocation of our need to grow and expand as a free Self.

This is not to say that all in-womb relationships have been positive for everyone. There is wide belief that we experience a lot in the womb. Studies of the brain have contended that the fetus is able to hear music and other sounds in the early months. It is widely believed the child is greatly impacted in negative ways before ever being born, if the mother is not stable, is involved with drugs or alcohol, is terribly stressed, or perhaps does not want the baby.

Today, we know that drinking or smoking during pregnancy (of course, smoking is always a risk) is not recommended. This can, in fact, in cases of alcoholism and/or binge drinking, create fetal alcohol syndrome, leaving the newborn child with irreparable damage. There are many who believe that much of what is diagnosed as ADD (Attention Deficit Disorder) may, in fact be caused by alcohol consumption during pregnancy. These kinds of negative relationships in the womb will not be cognitively remembered by the child but will impact the very being and nervous system. Like other issues that negatively affect the child after birth, this one can create a deep and profound sense of insecurity. The smaller the child, the more he/she is vulnerable to fear, because we feel small in reference to other beings.

The Self is born ready to grow and to move forward into self-realization. Thus, the relationship with your mother at birth is critical in forming the groundwork for the growth process. If you watch babies, even in early days and weeks after birth, you can see they are different. They don't look alike, nor act alike. This is the earliest view of the unique Self in its purest form, even though it already has been influenced by life with mother in the womb.

As I have gone over my life and childhood with a fine-tooth comb (over many years), I can see what personality I came in with and how it was affected early on by my mother. She was twenty-three years old when I was born, but had experienced a terribly dysfunctional childhood. She had been abandoned at one month old by her mother, to live her first seven years with her maternal grandmother's very dysfunctional family. She had grown up in constant fear for her well-being. At age seven, she was suddenly transported to another town far away from the family she knew as hers, back to her birth mother, two half brothers and an alcoholic stepfather, who were strangers to her.

The rest of my mother's childhood was miserable, as she experienced and witnessed physical, sexual, and emotional abuse, in addition to poverty. She had married at not quite eighteen, in hopes, I believe, of being taken care of and escaping the effects of poverty and the abuse of her childhood. But, the internal damage already was too deep. She waited five years to have me, her first child. She was very nervous, and had very mixed feelings about having a baby. I since have learned that she sometimes drank heavily in her twenties. No one cautioned about drinking during pregnancy in the 1940s. Also, in those days it was almost unheard of to choose NOT to have children, or she might have made that choice.

She, like many women of her generation and mine, were expected to have children. At best, I believe, my mother had a fantasy of a baby being like a little doll, which would be loveable and provide her with some of the love she had been deprived of by her mother, but certainly not the other way around, where she would need to provide the love and patience. She did not know how to do mothering, having received almost none herself.

As I came to know my mother in later years, it became evident how terribly fear- and shame-based she was and how much she was preoccupied with her body and possible pains and illnesses. Also, it became clear how much denial and how many memories she had repressed in her childhood to survive emotionally. She had formed some impossible fantasy of her childhood, no doubt to help her feel less shame, as the reality was too terrible to accept. It couldn't have been easy for her to go through pregnancy. Add to this, the fact that my dad was terrified that she would die in pregnancy, as his mother had, when he was only three. Both of my parents had severe issues of abandonment.

In addition to this, I have experienced and learned over the years how controlling my mother was by wanting conformity at all times and at all ages. Conforming keeps everyone in a predictable box in the hope to assure safety. It also stifles creativity and growing. An example is that she always claimed I was potty trained at six months of age! Though I don't doubt she tried (with great frustration for us both) and plenty of extreme early messages of failure for me, this is not something a six-month-old infant can do. Thus, I came into the world, probably after a somewhat tense ride in mother's womb, a baby with a very curious outgoing personality and high energy, but already with some fear. I came to a mother who was scared, scarred, externally preoccupied, and with great needs to control her family and environment, because she had experienced so little of this in her childhood. I came to a father, who carried his family's depression and was gone from our home working most of the time. Fear was a household theme in my home, not always visible but ever present. My parents had just come through The Great Depression, and World War II was in high gear when I was born.

There are many factors that no doubt affect a newborn's Self in relationship with the mother. Some of these would be what I have described as my entrance and pre-entrance to the world. Others would be such things as the following: whether the mother took care of herself physically, mentally, and emotionally; the status of her relationship with her mate — the father; her career; amount of worrying; focus on having a certain sexed child (boy or girl) and therefore disappointed with the child's gender; her feelings about having a baby in her body; drug use (including nicotine and/or prescription drugs) alcohol, excessive sugar; unresolved anger; other children to care for, or anxiety at this being the first; financial stability. All or any of these, along with many other conditions of the mother's relationship to herself and her world, will impact the infant in the womb and as a newborn.

The Self will emerge with some variation of feeling secure, to STAY INTACT, or begin to have trust issues. If there is birth with a fair amount of fear and anxiety for the infant, the relationship at birth already has become the first trauma in relationship to affect Self. An infant is totally helpless the first year, after which, with beginning to walk, to communicate a few words, and to feed itself, there begins to be a minimal break from total dependency.

There have been studies filming babies and how they respond to a female caregiver just using the positive behavior of smiling and then showing a blank face. Though I saw this film several years ago, it deeply impacted me to watch the child squirm and become visibly disturbed when the woman stopped smiling. This experiment was so simple, so seemingly small, yet it was evident how this interactive process, without words, had such a discomforting effect on the child. Imagine then, how it affects a child to be yelled at — or worse — to be hit.

More than once I have approached a parent of a young child (age one to three years old) in a store or other public place to suggest to the parent(s) that the child is too young to obey, to be chastised, or to be expected to conform to things it doesn't comprehend. I instinctively know, too, that this parent has been treated in the same way by their parents in their childhood. Seeing the shamed and frightened look on a child like this breaks my heart. They are experiencing emotional abuse, fraught with shaming messages, and learning that relationship is not safe. And, if a child perceives it isn't safe with Mom or Dad, then who could they ever be safe with? This can be the beginning of global thinking for the child, generalizing this experience to the whole world of one's future. Here begins fear of intimacy, which plagues so many people, who are unable to sustain relationship as an adult. Here begins fear to take risks and lowered self-esteem.

Here begins the visible effects of this child's "stewpot," as the relationship with the parents, often including extended family, begin to play upon the child's Self. These parents and relatives are passing on their relationship history to the child, flavoring and/or adding spoilage

Physical and emotional abandonments profoundly affect infants and small children, especially because they are not capable of caring for Self, or of understanding that the abandonment will end. Therefore, the trauma of this happens quickly and deeply in the Self of the child. As a newborn, the child becomes this extremely vulnerable entity with the shock of leaving the womb and with no control over its relationship to light, sound, smells, and touch. It is totally needy of constant connection to its mother or to other caretakers. Any show of negativity or perceived loss of its mother's presence is experienced with fear and anxiety, with no ability to reassure Self or know how to process this negativity and/or know that mother will reappear. I have found in clinical practice that changes of caregivers and/or loss of the birth mother or of the original mother figure during infancy can profoundly affect the child and his/her future ability to trust and connect. Sigmund Freud and Erik Erikson, in describing stages of development, speak of the formation of trust as being formed in early stages, from birth to age two. As the child is most vulnerable and dependent in infancy, they are referring to forming the most important foundation: trust. This first two-year mark also tells us a lot about problems in adoptions, especially those that do not occur right at birth. In addition, if there is divorce including joint custody, the child will experience the most abandonment in these early years, as this small child is unable to comprehend that the loss of one parent to the other is temporary, thus experiencing fear and loss as this agreement transpires.

Also, if there is shared custody in the child's early years where the child has managed to bond with both parents, and then one moves away, greatly lessening shared visits, it can be traumatizing for the child. This was the case with Manny, who had shared time with his mom and dad. He adored his dad, and he became hysterical and angry when he was informed that his dad was moving away. This was so traumatic that Manny had repressed the memory until it came up in therapy.

Infancy is the most vulnerable state we experience, and, therefore, we have the most need to trust that we will be safe. Don't think a baby doesn't experience a difference in the transfer from the birth mother to a stranger. When adoptions are delayed or the child is shifted from one caregiver to another before being settled into a permanent home, there is bound to be a deep violation of trust. This lack of trust, however, cannot be verbalized but will be reflected in defensive behaviors, such as a baby being overly fussy because it is fearful. Troublesome older adoptees are probably most reflecting fear from having been handed around, perhaps multiple times with multiple disappointments, and have learned to defend themselves with adverse behaviors to try to avoid disappointment. Their experience tells them, "I know you will reject me, so let's get it over with. No one wants me."

One woman I worked with discovered that she had been (through adoption process) handed around to three potential mothers in her first three months of life. Throughout her adult life, she has had profound trust and abandonment issues and a good amount of paranoia about people. Recapturing this kind of trauma to work past it is very difficult when the trauma comes from infancy. Many adopted children suffer trauma from the loss of birth mother, which leaves an early film of mistrust and insecurity. It is very important that the adopting parents handle this subject with great care, because there is already relationship crisis.

Someone else I have known suffered years of isolation and loneliness, afraid to get close to people. Her mother told her as an adult that she didn't like to be held even when she was a baby. As this woman explored her family of origin, she realized that the truth no doubt was that she was afraid of her caregivers early on, as they were unpredictable, alcoholic, and would often hit her, as soon as hold her. She realized that she learned to fear contact as a small baby, which explained why she didn't like to be held. In fact, she discovered that she always had been starved to be held and touched but was too afraid of people after her early relationship experience to get close to anyone.

I also have learned some things about my infancy from relatives that have helped explain some of my anxieties that continued into adulthood. My aunt shared that my mother left me with her for two weeks when I was six weeks old, while she traveled to attend her mother's funeral. She shared that to appease me and to be able to sleep, I needed to sleep with her, which is understandable for an infant, whose mother has disappeared. Although it is quite understandable that my mother would have to leave me —

sometimes it is unavoidable — the part that struck me as very telling about my mother's mothering was that my aunt said she had to keep it a secret from my mother, because she would have disapproved — another (of many) indications that my mother was unable to understand or nurture a child.

My sister also has experienced a lot of fallout from, among other things, being sent out of town to a hospital for three weeks early in her infancy, because she could not digest milk. Again, this could not be avoided back in those days, but that early isolation from our mother, followed by numerous other emotional abandonments, deeply has affected her throughout her life in her relationships. There are few things that impact us as heavily as experienced abandonment. In my childhood, my mother would sometimes sneak out to the movies (so my father wouldn't know, as his religion was against movies) and leave me in my crib for a nap. I remember waking up and screaming for her, but she wasn't there. It seemed like an eternity. My mother never understood that a small child cannot just be told, "I'll be back soon." Sadly, I left my own two-year-old daughter with a relative for a week and was told she watched the window for me to return every day. I wish I had known better then, about how we repeat traumatic experiences. I feel great sadness still, when I imagine my daughter at that window.

The most devastating way in which my mother abandoned me was by emotionally cutting me off and not speaking to me for days or weeks when she was displeased. Physical, verbal, and sexual abuse create the most deep and lasting scars when inflicted on an infant. I have no doubt that I suffered verbal abuse from the time I was born, because it was her major, constant communication with me throughout my entire life. She had no understanding of a child's inability to learn right from wrong or what is appropriate at early ages. She was one of those parents who would verbally hammer a little one to "act your age," when, in fact, you were acting your age — of three. My aunt also told me that she witnessed my mother hitting me with a belt in the crib when I wouldn't stop crying.

For me, this explained a lot about my life of high anxiety. Early relationships, even as an infant, have profound effects.

I fared better in some ways with my father. I know that he adored me as a small child, that the sun rose and set with me, and, most importantly, he loved my high energy and was patient with me. I know that he delighted in me. He was basically a very gentle man, so there were no angry reactions to an infant from him. But, he worked long hours and was not there for the daily work and attention needed by an infant, or to protect me from an over-controlling and often unsafe mother. As was true throughout my childhood, he did not know how very impatient and overwhelmed my mother was all the time and therefore not a healthy nurturer. However, in his disease of alcoholism, my father also began to be inappropriate with me at a very young age. This means he abandoned me as a father, and put me in the role of a lover. It profoundly affected my relationship with him, with my mother, and with all my adult love relationships. Because I repressed these memories of incest, I kept a conscious fantasy of him as the good parent and my mother (who was angry, controlling and verbally abusive) as the bad parent. He also would give me almost anything I wanted well into my adulthood, and when I remembered the violation of our father-daughter relationship, I realized much of this excessive giving was coming from his guilt. As I recovered my memories I realized that my symptoms, such as waking up at night and thinking someone was standing beside my bed, fearing a light that could be seen under a door, (this would be when my father was roaming around drunk in the middle of the night), having to be very covered up at night regardless of the temperature, and later attracting sexual behaviors that I did not like, when I was intoxicated as an adult, was evidence of the sexual abuse. It also became clear why I moved downstairs in my house at age twelve to a room that would be safer, as the creaky steps would forewarn me if my father was coming in the night. I would stay up very late at night, unaware it was because I was fearful and being vigilant.

This ability for one to repress memories has been the subject of some controversy in recent years. I can tell you that it is real and have seen it not only in myself, but also in clients. In many cases, including mine, it has been discovered by noting the symptomatic behaviors one displays that is fallout from abuse. I learned that my father was not the good one and my mother not the bad one, but that they were a combination of two wounded people, who repeated abuses onto their children. However, knowing this did not heal my wounds. It took more years of therapy to let go and forgive.

Starting in infancy, parents' emotional conditions, relationship with each other, and their family-of-origin history are major factors in forming a child's well-being. Again, when you look at my parents' families of origin, it is easier to see reasons for the ways in which they behaved. My mother suffered numerous physical and emotional abandonments, often because of the financial stresses of her family in the early 1900s, thus creating tremendous insecurity in her own Self and making it understandable that she would believe that having enough money and things was the answer to a good life. My dad also grew up poor as the descendant of six generations of families, who worked other people's land in this country until they finally began to acquire some of their own, just in my father's lifetime. His childhood, during the early 1900s, was fraught with trauma of the 1918 flu, which took his mother's life when he was three, leaving his thirteen-year-old sister to mother him and his two other siblings, until she also left him at age sixteen to get married. His family also was moving frequently from state to state in Appalachia for his dad to find work. He had to quit school in the seventh grade to go to work, to help support the family.

My parents' early marital relationship was fraught with my mother's fears of being poor, and they both drank a lot. A major difference in their backgrounds was religion; my father grew up in a Christian fundamentalist family, and my mother's family did not practice a religion, though her grandmother, with whom she spent her first seven years, was also a Christian fundamentalist. This meant that she was much more liberal in her life than was Dad's family. They lived with his family until I was born and then moved nearby.

Since my first grandson was born nine years ago, I have gained incredible awareness about the precious vulnerability of an infant. I have been in awe watching the excitement of my son and daughter-in-law, as they have so much patience, love, and focus on learning to be good parents. I also have been in awe in watching both of my grandsons in those first few weeks, then months, so dependent on their relationship with their mother, so incredibly needy for gentleness, patience, and love, and then watching them be so responsive to the outpouring of this from my daughter-in-law and son. I wish that I could have been a healthier mother to my four babies. But, I am so impressed by my son and his wife in their commitment to healing their "Family Stew" issues, making them available as healthy, nurturing parents. Watching all of them smile and laugh in response to so much love has been one of the greatest joys of my life. All of this is happening in relationship and all greatly forming their future relationships.

Questionnaire on Relationship at Birth and Infancy

1. Write a paragraph or more describing what you know about your birth, the circumstances of your family/parents when you were born, what number child you were, how you think your parents felt about having you, and any other details you know that may be very significant around your birth. Include relatives who were involved.

2. Are you adopted? Are any of your siblings or your parents adopted? Write about this. Were you given to a relative, nanny, neighbor, or other person during your first three years for some period of time, such as when your parents were away or during a financial situation, etc.?

3. What kind of personality do you think you entered into world with? Out-going? Subdued?

Chapter Two

RELATIONSHIP WITH OUR FAMILY OF ORIGIN ADAPTIVE ROLES

How we get lost in the stew

Following our experience in the womb, family of origin is where our most profound, impactful, and long-lasting experiences with relationship begin and significantly form us for the rest of our lives. Relationships become the machinery that operates the family system. We begin our journey absorbing our "Family Stew."

Each person or piece of the family must work in sync to have any kind of a working family system, be it functional or dysfunctional. Each child, as another component or piece added to the family system, must find a way to fit in — a way to feel loved and special. In dysfunctional families, children take on adaptive roles to do this. What we believe about our Self comes from what we believe our parents think and feel about us, which can make or break us emotionally. This belief can help us to move forward in life or leave us stuck emotionally, where we give up or drive ourselves forever to try to achieve the approval we always have wanted, but never received from our parents.

Dysfunctional family behaviors and patterns in adult life come from not leaving home emotionally, meaning our family of origin. Many therapists do not spend much time exploring family of origin with their clients. This deeply concerns me, as it is from the early childhood relationships with authority figures — even if it is reactionary to our parents — that we form most of our belief system. This includes what we believe about our Self, our self-esteem, our behaviors, our concepts of male and female, our ability to take risks, and, most of all, how we will function in our animate and inanimate relationships. In fact, these relationships, to varying degrees, will determine how we experience and function in the world and with those in it, and how we choose our most important relationships.

Therefore, examining our family of origin and our childhood years gives us the tools to become aware of ourselves, and how and why we function the way we do in relationships. It is invaluable to do this in couples' work, because we carry our family of origin deep in our being for all of our lives, and mates and close relationships involve transferences of our early caregivers and the household themes we experienced. What is to be discovered are the beliefs, behaviors, and themes we have taken on while adapting or surviving our childhood, which ones are really our choice, and whether they are working for us in our adult life.

All of these secrets to our awareness can be revealed in an in-depth exploration of our family of origin. Many people have the attitude of "that is in the past, leave it there." No, it is definitely not in the past, for it lives within us in our ideas about life, in our behaviors and in our relationships every day. If one feels trapped in the inability to have relationships, the answer lies in family of origin with what baggage is being carried from our childhood and what is unfinished business. It is usually not an easy path to explore, it is often painful, and it often takes time, but it always will yield the opening of doors to healthier relationships and many, many more choices.

Though cognitive and behavioral therapy often are good adjunct tools, if used alone or without in-depth emotional work and without a look at one's history for traumas, people, or events that are probably related to the presenting problem (especially if it is a recurring pattern), these therapies will not be enough for a person to make real and lasting changes to enhance their life and relationships.

Freud was right. The first six years of our life are the most critical years in forming how we will survive and interact in relationship with the world. Freud did, however, limit stages of development to the early years. Erik Erikson went on to define eight stages of development, showing that it continues throughout our life into old age. His work shows how poor resolution of our stages of development continues to impact our relationships as we age. His work is very worth reading. I saw a film in graduate school that was made about these stages, which wonderfully depicts his concepts. With all the years of study in psychology, no one has succeeded in contradicting the incredible impact of early childhood, which is about relationships.

When we are born, we have no ideas about anything. We have not developed the ability to think. We are only capable of experiencing. However, we certainly do sense the difference between positive and negative energy and behaviors around us. In our youngest years, we are the most open and sensitive to stimuli that we will ever be.

As I continue to write about the impacts of relationship I will give many specific examples. However, the old belief that children are resilient, often meaning or implying that they can survive anything, has much truth in it. It is true that most of us are incredible survivors of many things, even severe traumas. It is not true that it is without scars. The scars or wounds, as I will refer to them throughout this book, are what impact our future relationships and how we navigate life. It varies how we adapt to these wounds, but it is in this process of adapting that we hide our true Self, forming distorted views and skills in relationship. I will discuss this concept of roles and splits by discussing the Adaptive Self, which I find particularly effective in helping people find a way back to a healthy true Self, often referred to as the inner child, who has been frozen inside a wounded child.

The Adaptive Self is something we form somewhere in our childhood when we are traumatized or just don't feel safe. We form adaptive parts of Self when we become fear and/or shame based. We form this for protection, to try to find a meaningful place in the family, to avoid being shamed, and to get the nurture and affirmations we so desperately need as children. This Adaptive Self (or in some cases Adaptive Selves) is also a defensive Self, formed to try to protect the wounded Self, and be able to function in an unsafe environment without the benefit of sufficient guidance.

My father adored me when I was very small and the only child. He went too far, violating important boundaries. Even though she wasn't aware of these violations, my mother was jealous of his attention. She had been so deprived as a child, she could not even share him with his daughters.

I was extremely precocious, curious, and highly active. As a result of my mother's feelings about me and her jealousy of my relationship with my dad, she rejected me and was highly critical. Then, as a small child, I adapted by becoming more difficult to handle and finding ways to upset her, which actually made me feel, in this Adaptive Self, very powerful, though it also brought me more shame and punishments from her reactions to me.

But, remember, a child will do anything to connect to a parent — anything to not be ignored. My behavior guaranteed attention from her. She was the classic co-dependent wife of an alcoholic and obsessed with my dad. I got whatever I wanted materially from my dad and was very defiant toward her. I convinced myself that I did not care what she thought (never true) and proceeded to prove her wrong about me in every way that I could. Whatever she said about me I proved the opposite, though it was a losing battle, because she never would affirm me. I adapted in this way, storing away a wounded child, who was devastated by betrayals of both parents. I acted as if I was fine and could conquer the world. I played this role so well, that at age fifteen, when I was sharing with my girlfriend about how unhappy I felt inside, she was astounded! She said, "But you have everything. You are pretty and popular and do well at everything!" Yes, those were the external truths. Inside, I hated myself, because behind closed doors in my home, my mother seemed to hate me, and my father by now was not safe at night and had become distant and only concerned that I not upset my mother. The successes and affirmations in my outside life did not touch my needs to have the safety and approval of my parents. Also, it was very "crazy making", as it did not make sense why my mother was not proud of me and why everything successful that I did seemed somehow to make me more of a burden. In this way, I ended up falling into two dysfunctional roles: scapegoat and hero child. I was mother's scapegoat at home. In the outside world at school and community events, I excelled as the hero of the family, attempting to prove to Mom how good I was.

Meanwhile, my sister, born eight years after me, formed an Adaptive Self, who, isolated, avoided family conflict and was compliant with Mother to form a less conflicted relationship than mine. She was our lost child. In this way, forming an adaptive child is a splitting off of and taking on an acting role, which eventually behaves as the Self. There are many problems with this. First, it is not the true Self, which is the real core of whom you are at birth. This is stowed away when you adapt, and the adapting is for survival, not for growth and self-actualization. Secondly, and unfortunately, when we form an Adaptive Self, we are not aware that this is not our true Self, and, unlike acting in a play, the adaptive roles do not go away when the family-of-origin play is over. We go right out into adult life as the Adaptive Self, or, for some, the Adaptive Selves.

Another problem about the adaptive child is that even as a grownup, she/he is living out of this adaptation of a self- protector with mostly only the skills of a child. Relationship skills come from home — where, as in my case, they were hurtful. This does not help a lot in grownup life and in relationships. Adapting always involves dysfunctional behaviors, such as manipulation and dishonesty. Any and all these behaviors are about survival. So, after helping one survive, this Adaptive Self tends to be inept at adult life and keeps wounding the inner self more, reinforcing low self-esteem and feelings of un-lovability. One of the most important ways this reinforcement happens is in relationships that are chosen.

In my case, part of my adapting was to be grandiose and overconfident to compensate for feeling inadequate from my parents' rejections. Others might reflect low self-esteem by retreating into themselves. I learned to manipulate adults with charm and feminine wiles. Thus, as a grownup, I sometimes would barge into situations or people and often make a fool of myself, only to experience another rejection. This intruding was a behavior of my mother's that I hated. On the other hand, not to completely malign my adaptive child, her style made me a fearless risk taker, persistent in my determination to achieve my goals. Sadly, until recovery, this drive was still internally motivated by wanting my parents' approval and love through many, hopeless transferences. There was no real sense of entitlement in my wounded Self, no amount of success will ever be enough if you don't believe in your Self. This was my style of still playing out my adaptive role of the family hero as a grownup, until I worked on healing emotionally.

Another way of looking at our Adaptive Self is by the role descriptions of children in dysfunctional families. I see these roles as part of our adaptive child. This is the second part of how we lose or store away the real Self, in taking on roles in the dysfunctional family. The following roles were first, to my knowledge, described by Sharon Wegscheider-Cruse in a pamphlet called "The Family Trap." The family is a connected operating system, and where there is dysfunction there is uncertainty, lack of stability, a general lack of.

The first role in the family, often taken on by the oldest child, as in my case, is that of family hero. In this role, the child often plays a role reversal with one of the parents, meaning she/he behaves as parent to the parent. This role usually includes excelling outside the home, such as in athletics or academics, winning leadership roles at school, etc. This is the child's attempt to hide dysfunction in the family, such as alcoholism, domestic abuse, embarrassing moments, or practices of the parents. At home, it is an attempt to stabilize the house, be loved for being useful, or sometimes to take care of the other children. This role in very large families may be repeated again and again, as are the other roles.

The next role, most often adapted by the second child, is that of scapegoat, but roles can come in any birth order. This role is the defiant role. The scapegoat can be likened to a dump, where undesirable items are thrown. It is a place to load whatever negativity and blame the parents are unwilling to face, such as fear of their own (adaptive) personalities, inappropriate behaviors, self- shame, addictions, and other problems in the family. Since the good guy/caretaker role already is taken, this second child falls vulnerable to this role and learns to become the scapegoat with his or her behaviors only noticed when negative. The scapegoat will grow up with real self hate. And, yes, we are taught by how the parents react or respond, by trial and error to play our roles.

Sometimes we see the third child, or another, take on the role of lost child. This child usually has a more shy personality, is more avoidant than the hero or scapegoat, and is a people watcher. This child's motto would be some version of "Get me out of here!" And, in the purest form, the lost child will avoid the family as much as possible, by being gone a lot or in their room reading alone. They grow up feeling very neglected and learn to deeply distrust people. They often become isolators.

The fourth role, often adapted by the youngest child, is that of family mascot. The mascot really does not know where to fit in, develops a good bit of hyper behavior, makes little problems, and displays inappropriate behaviors that are interruptive to bring attention to Self. I believe that some children are misdiagnosed as hyper active as a medical condition, where really they have adapted the mascot role. The mascot is terribly insecure and often uses humor to hide feelings or to distract from painful situations. The mascot often will be the most immature adult and is often at the most risk for suicide. Comedians are a great example of mascots.

Many of us play more than one of these roles in the family. I did, as hero and scapegoat. My sister was a lost child, with a secondary role of mascot. I was always more prominently in the hero role outside my home. Naturally, when I married and was making my own home, I fell into a scapegoat role with my husband, who, as I said before, was much like my mother. Our marital relationship was negative and combative, just as both our relationships had been with our mothers as children.

One of my clients, Barbara, grew up in what looked like a healthy, functional home. However, it was a looking-good family, who were emotionally shut down, except for Barbara. Her three sisters adapted to the intellectual theme that dominated the family, but Barbara was extremely emotional and was therefore the scapegoat. Her parents were clearly afraid of emotions and gave her messages that something was wrong with her. As a result, her self-esteem hit rock bottom. She always felt like the oddball child. The parents' rejection was subtle and verbal. It was their remarks and concern that they expressed about how she, unlike her siblings, did not adapt to the family theme of intellectualism. She began doing drugs early in high school and developed a defiant, adaptive child. She would not attempt intellectual pursuits, such as a college degree or a professional career. She developed a wild side, and, though just as bright as her parents and siblings, she could not let herself pursue a career where her extraordinary creative abilities could be shared and enjoyed. She wrote beautiful poetry and sometimes did very creative and effective things with children. But, her family never affirmed her for this and she grew up afraid to use these abilities, believing she was a failure and a misfit.

Bill's parents divorced when he was small, leaving his mother with four children and the need to work long hours. His dad, though well off financially, did not provide much money for the family. Bill experienced a lot of abandonment from his dad leaving and also because his mom worked and dated a lot. There was never much money. Bill became a scapegoat as a child and a hero later in life. He was very angry and driven to be successful to prove how good he was. He did drugs in high school and college, until he sought help. He had adapted to become grandiose, making a good deal of money, but nothing was enough. He was trying to gain self-esteem by looking good and becoming successful in his profession. This, of course, does not work, because to regain self-esteem, it becomes an inside job, not an outside one.

Barbara's and Bill's stories are only two of many, but you will find people's stories in all of my chapters, and they all involve loss of self-esteem in whatever subjects I give examples.

One of the saddest things about our adaptation in these ways is that we continue to go through life as an actor. We are, in fact, like a spider caught in the web of our parents, our ancestors, and all their stuff, and our wounds and defenses have been formed from all of this! We feel strangely unfulfilled and try to fill the void with all sorts of external people, places, substances, and things. We try drugs, fancy cars and houses, power careers, food, shopping, sex, gambling, money, and more. Yet, because it is the true Self and the love of it that we are missing, none of this works. Saddest of all, these efforts to fill this void continue the abusive and rejecting behaviors toward the true Self. Real value of Self and self-care is not something we are even aware of as adult children, and we therefore tend to not nurture and do healthy things for ourselves.

There is a truckload of possibilities for relationship lessons in the early years. These include the caregivers, particularly Mom and Dad (present or not), and any other relatives, neighbors, nannies, babysitters, foster parents, and siblings. Although the majority of children spend some or most of the early years with one or both parents, many children grow up primarily with grandparents, other relatives, or with one or more nannies. Also, many children today spend most of their daytime hours in daycare centers. All of these relationships become part of who the child becomes. There is no absolute answer as to which type of caregivers will do the best job because, for example, not all parents are emotionally healthy. Sometimes a child may get more nurturing and safety in a foster home than with, for example, drug addicted, out-of-control parents, or terribly angry, verbally abusive parents. The legal system, where children are the concern, is supposed to be there for the child's best interest but too often fails to accomplish this.

We are still a long way from making nurturing, emotional safety, and stability the main factors that decide where a child in question is placed. It was well into the Twentieth Century before children in Europe and America stopped being used for child labor. It is really only in the past thirty years or so that children are beginning to be considered people with rights.

The most important factors of successful care-giving have to do with the caregivers' emotional and mental health. It requires emotional maturity, having a well-defined Self, and being available to provide a safe, nurturing environment in which the child can feel secure and grow. Each of us has a set of circumstances surrounded by caregivers and others that forms our own experience, belief system, and ability to function in relationship with people, places, and things.

I work with many people from all sorts of backgrounds and relationship experiences, and I compare my childhood. I had a terribly insecure mother, who was intensely critical of me. And, I had a mostly unavailable father, who molested me and was rarely my protector. However, they did provide physical, environmental safety through nice homes and other financial advantages, which enabled me to be the first in either of their families to attend college and to develop a life with more opportunities to expand my horizons. Although, most importantly, I suffered constant emotional abuse, I have found that my parents, who never divorced nor threatened it, did many things that facilitated my making it in the world.

I have worked with people who grew up in poverty, came from broken homes with constant moving, and who lacked most physical necessities, in addition to the emotional and other abuses that I suffered. This has made me realize that I did get some gifts from those two people, who were so terribly wounded themselves. Having grown up in poverty, my parents figured the way to happiness was to have money and things, to stay together, and to look good at all costs. Though it does add to one's life stability, it certainly is only the icing on the cake. It is not the cake. The cake is emotional security and a true sense of Self.

Most parents, except those who are truly mentally ill, try to do their best. Sometimes people get an incorrect view about why we do family-of-origin work, thinking it is just about blaming our parents and not taking our own responsibility. This is not the reason for following this path to emotional recovery. The reason, as I stated earlier, is to gain more awareness of who we are and why we behave in the ways that we do. It is to examine this and our belief systems, carried from childhood, decide if they are working for us and whether we choose to change them. Sometimes in the process, we do have to work through some anger at our parents for what we experienced and how that has affected us. We need to recognize where our dysfunction comes from. In emotional expressive work, we give back what does not belong to us. Our parents need not be present.

It is very healing just to find out that there are reasons for being the way I am and that I'm not crazy. In going back and exploring, we need to recognize that we are not responsible for our parents' misdeeds. We call it "giving back the shame." As children, we almost always think their behaviors toward us are about us (and sometimes they say it is), and where there are dysfunctional caregivers, we take on a lot of shame about Self that does not belong to Self. Another thing we do is form a distorted view of who our parents are, whether it is to whitewash them as saints, or dark wash them as bad. Often we have a view of one good parent and one bad parent. Neither is true. We are all a mixed bag. To see ourselves and others clearly, we need to sort out who our parents or caregivers really were as human beings — positive and negative. Also in a full inventory of our history and parenting, we need to note the positives we experienced that contributed to who we are, such as I noted earlier about the physical comforts and opportunities that my parents provided for me.

CHILDHOOD DECISIONS & SELF-FULFILLING PROPHECIES

In family of origin, we learn our most deeply believed lessons about life and often make profound decisions that continue to guide our path for years or for a lifetime, if we don't become aware of them. Awareness gives us the ability to change. These decisions usually are not remembered but live in us at an unconscious level, buried in the wounded child part of us. Prejudice and bias often are part of this and are hard to shake off, even with experience to the contrary. These decisions can be made from a family theme, such as conflict around money, or from an incident in young life that has a traumatic effect. How they become evident is in what we come to recognize as our theme(s) in life, which we manifest as an adult. An example of this is making a decision never to marry because of being traumatized as a child, while constantly hearing threats of divorce or statements such as, "I should never have married you!" Or, knowing a parent is unfaithful and seeing the pain this creates is interpreted by the child as hopelessness with respect to marriage, rather than the dysfunction within the particular marital relationship.

This unconsciousness of what we are up to often creates a lot of pain. For example, the very emotional fear that a decision was made to avoid, leaves us walking through life much like a blind or very seeing-impaired person. In a case such as this, forming a small child conclusion that marriage creates the pain, one can end up unable to commit to another and end up isolated.

Nina was traumatized at age eight when her father had an affair with a relative. How she dealt with the shame and trauma of this was in forming her private logic, concluding that the cause of this pain was the institution of marriage. As time passed, she continued to collect evidence of this while watching her relatives and neighbors and seeing a lot of conflict and struggles in marriages. There was a lot of alcoholism in her extended family. As a result, she has not married. Though she has had two long-term relationships, she becomes frozen in fear at the mention of marriage.

Interestingly, her sister Susan has done the exact same thing with respect to college. Already full of self-doubt from being ignored and criticized by her caretakers, Susan made a decision to not even try to attend a regular university, as she had dreamed about, because her stepmother told her there would be no way she could attend without money. Sadly, the truth was and is that there is lots of money to be found in scholarships and student loans. Susan just gave up, made a decision that was not based on available facts, and also believed she was not worth it anyway. This decision caused her to feel even more inadequate as she matured into her twenties, because a lack of a college education made her feel like an outsider and limited in her possibilities.

Another example is a decision that "money only creates pain, so it will have no importance to me." I know someone who, through listening to arguments between her parents about money on a regular basis, decided that money was what caused such painful disagreements, and, therefore, it would never be important to her. This decision has kept this person in pain concerning money throughout her adult life, because it is a necessary part of life, of course. By giving money no importance she has been insecure, unable to provide for herself and for her family, and constantly struggles in relationship with family. Thus, we have an example of self-fulfilling prophecies, where "money only creates pain." Again, what originally created the pain that this child experienced was the parents' inability to handle money, not the money itself.

A child cannot process this, so the child isolates the concept of money as problem. This and such decisions that are made by a child, often as young as three, are based on the very limited experience of his/her own family of origin. And, such a decision could happen from a general theme of struggle and pain around money that goes on for a number of years, or it could be a struggle that only exists for a short time when the child is vulnerable and traumatized around it. These decisions are made out of the private logic that a child forms in an unsafe household. The decisions seem to make no sense or cannot be explained in adulthood, until one goes back and finds the childhood root, or the emotional root of this belief.

When we are little, so are our skills at figuring things out — little and limited. As children, we always think we can do it differently, until we grow up and find out that we just repeat our caregivers' dysfunctions almost exactly, or get the same result by attempting to do the opposite. For example, over controlling or protecting a child, not letting him take risks or be creative, creates the same insecurity that is created by neglect and non-involvement. Neither child will have self-confidence. Money or financial management is a huge and important issue in growing up and is dysfunctional in many families.

Certainly some of the most important conclusions drawn by children, when they are not equipped to do this, are about men and women. If the mother and/or other female caregivers are submissive, this is role modeling for a girl about how to be in a relationship. It can also be a son, who is impacted by this, depending on personality and other relationships in the household. The daughter will either follow the same style, or if rebellious, will "make sure I am never anything like that" and be overly

Anne Salter, LCSW

independent. Both women will have trouble in relationship; one because she submits most of the time, the other because she can never yield. If the father is very successful and never available, his son may follow in his footsteps, even though he went through great pain missing his absent dad. Or, he may decide that success means pain (another life decision made by a child), so he won't ever be successful. In this case, the son (or daughter) may not even realize as an adult why he/she cannot seem to achieve success. It is because the decision is part of the unconscious and was made by a child. Of course, it was not the father's success that caused the pain. It was the father's inability to set priorities and to set boundaries with his work time, to be more available.

These conclusions that we come to often become generalized to the female and male population. For example, if the mother is experienced as cold and withholding, a child can grow up viewing females in this fashion, always picking females that exhibit some or a lot of this type of behavior, therefore continuing to have problems in relationship with females and having unmet needs, creating a self-fulfilling prophesy.

Children make black-and-white decisions: extremes. They are not ready to make such grandiose decisions about life, but they make them out of a defense against fear of becoming something they see as dangerous or painful. I will give many more examples of decisions made in childhood and how they become self-fulfilling prophecies, become generalized to the whole world, and have profound impact on relationships.

Note: Questions relating to this chapter are at the end of Chapter 4.

Chapter Three

RELATIONSHIP WITH THE THEMES IN OUR FAMILY OF ORIGIN

It is reflected in our choices in all areas of our life

There are many possible themes in families. For example, themes such as stressing education, parents and/or grandparents who are consistent in their nurturing and setting of boundaries while open to creativity usually will have a very positive effect on children growing up. Unfortunately, many of us have experienced less positive themes, or some of the above was over ridden by more negative or abusive themes.

One of the most hurtful and damaging themes that prevents children from developing a healthy Self is the theme of addiction. Many people (far more than statistics imply) have either experienced addiction, lived with it as an adult, been attracted to those with it, and/or grew up in a family with addiction in one or many forms. Simplistically, when one is addicted, it is the main focus in their life. This is not because they are a bad person or want this to be the case, but because that is how the mental illness of addiction operates. Addiction is an obsessive behavior, whether all the time or only periodically. The addictive or addicted person always has a large part of available energy consumed with finding a way to avoid the internal pain they are carrying in their wounded baggage compartment.

As a theme in the family, it means that the addict and their addiction will take center stage in the daily life of the family. In other words, the addiction is the central focus of the addicted person, and they in turn become the central focus in the family. The addictive disease has an actual relationship with the entire family, setting into action certain definable and predictable dynamics for everyone. That is why it's considered a family disease. Relationships are altered to adapt to the addiction. Spouse and/or children always try to find ways to stop it, control it, or manage it. Whether the addicted person is mood altered or not, or how often, is by far not the only criteria of the effects of addictions on relationship. Other dynamics that go on in the family as part of the addictive process are arguing, chaos, abandonments, financial difficulties, a lot of verbal abuse and blaming, and sometimes multiple addictions, including sex. If there is sexual abuse and/or incest, it will create lifelong impacts on relationships.

Usually the addiction disease theme stretches back one or several generations, so that in exploring one's family-of-origin history, there are often revelations such as, "Gee, grandma was a food addict," or "Now I see that grandpa was an alcoholic womanizer, so no wonder Mom left home at fifteen. I can see how that contributed to who she is and how she does relationship." Or, "All of mother's brothers were alcoholics." Or, "I see now that Uncle Bob was a sex addict." These are just a very few of the possibilities. Besides parents and grandparents, there are uncles and aunts and their spouses, cousins, great grandparents, stepparents and stepgrandparents, etc. Look at how many in the family have smoked and how many were/are workaholics and/or overeaters. Look at those with diabetes, who are overweight, yet still abuse sugar/food. Look at stories of grandpa's womanizing or affair(s), or grandma's. Look at family history where there were financial struggles in relationship, such as gambling and over-spending.

Also, look at any family history of depression, mental illness, and/or suicide.

Alcoholic and other addicted families do a lot of blaming. As a result of this, children often blame themselves for "Daddy's drinking." When I worked in an alcohol rehab center years ago, I remember a young, sixtee- year-old girl, whose father came to treatment in late-stage alcoholism with advanced liver disease. This young girl had come to believe that she was responsible for her dad's drinking, because she had poor posture, about which he always complained. I also have worked with many parents who blamed themselves for their children's addictions and then continue to support them as grown adults out of guilt. This just enables more addiction and other failures for this young person.

Besides its effects on relationship in the family, addiction keeps passing on to the children, and their children, and theirs. Basically children of alcoholics, food addicts, sex addicts, nicotine addicts, gambling or other money-addiction problems, rageaholics, workaholics, or relationship addicts, either marry an addict of some type, become one, or both. Most addicts also tend to have multiple addictions. The value of stopping this generational continuation of addiction disease is priceless in terms of having healthy relationships and fullness of individual life possibilities.

Chronic physical or mental illness is a major focus issue in some families, which creates many of the same dynamics as addiction. In addition, it very often underlies addiction. Today, there are many addicts who are given a dual diagnosis. Having a family member ill for a long time or always fragile from an earlier illness will cause family to revolve largely around that ill family member. This person, just like the addict, gets more focus and attention than anyone else in the family. If this person is a parent, it creates a great loss of parenting for the children, because focus, time, and resources of the other parent go to the one who is handicapped. I have worked with quite a number of adults, who come to recognize that even though there was plenty of money, physical comforts, and no threats of divorce, their self-esteem was greatly destroyed by the fact that focus was almost all on a sibling who was physically ill or had some form of handicap. They realize that this is truly a major form of emotional abandonment but had interpreted it to mean that their Self had very little value, which, of course, had affected their entire life in adverse ways. Naturally, it also precluded being guided and instructed in many important areas, so that private logic became more necessary to find answers. This is true in varying degrees for any kind of handicap.

In a family I know, there is an autistic child. Raising this child at home has required that she always be the priority. Both parents, especially the mother, are there first for this child, with whom there are constant crises requiring most of their emotional resources and money. This takes a huge toll on the other children, as they are often required to give up activities, time, and material things they might want. This has created a pattern of crises with the other four children, as it is a way to get attention. These children have learned to value this sadly handicapped child as the only, really special child. They were expected to continue the care of this severely handicapped child in the event of the mother's death, until recently, when the mother began to realize the extent of the toll this was taking on the other children. This, of course, would impact their ability to have a life in general and to find a mate who would want to take on such a heavy, lifelong responsibility. Fortunately, this mother, as she gains more awareness and recovery from her codependency, already has begun to make other arrangements. Parents who do this do not mean to neglect the other children or to make them feel not special, but that is the real fallout from this situation. The other children get unintentionally cheated.

Another example of a problem, where there is a central person or thing that eats up the caregiver's focus, can be the death of a family member, who is not mourned together with the children and who seems to forever remain the most important family member. The other children, especially if this was a sibling who was perceived as the parents' hero, will feel tremendous guilt, some

Anne Salter, LCSW

anger, and often try all sorts of ways to somehow take on the role of this dead person. This is an attempt to fill the void and to bond with the parents.

I knew a young man whose brother was killed in a motorcycle accident. His brother, two years older than him, was the family hero. He was the star athlete, the academic high achiever, everything that made this family feel proud and look good. He was gone. The parents were devastated but never mourned him with their other two children. This young man, the next son in birth order, had never felt special. Besides this towering older brother, who was clearly Dad's favorite, his little sister was closer to his mother.

Soon after his brother was killed, Dom began to plan his future. He would make up for the loss of his brother to make his parents happy. Without realizing it, he had made a child's decision to try to become his brother, as a way to be special. Thus, he began to work hard at being a star for his parents. He tried to compete with the memory of a dead brother, who, of course, had become the fantasy symbol of what would have been a perfect person, bringing great esteem to the family. Dom set out to do this impossible task, which meant never once considering who his true Self might be, what his own goals might have been. Tragically, this path was destined only to bring him pain. Sadder still, he did not realize that this was what he was doing and was not aware of its roots. He was in burn-out mode, because he had no relationship with his true Self. We can never become someone else, fill the place of a sibling, or live up to an impossible fantasy of perfection. This central savior-figure focus in this family created no place for Dom, or for his sister to bloom and grow into their own Self path.

Having any kind of handicapped person in the family often creates this person as a central focus. Whatever the handicap, the family must adapt to it. Besides some form of mental retardation, there are many other possible physical handicaps at birth, or that occur during childhood, such as the autism I described earlier.

I remember the polio epidemic that happened in my hometown when I was a child and knowing families who had a child stricken with polio. It changed their family life and dynamics drastically, as everyone had to realign in the family system to the sick child. Or, in some cases, they had to mourn the death of a child. For the stricken child, this was not only a major trauma that changed expected life possibilities but also was a major loss physically. For the siblings, there was loss of the security of a physically healthy family, where the parents' attention was more equally shared. Everyone had to deal with the fear and adapt to the loss of a relationship as they had known it.

When a child is born with some form of physical handicap, there is a burden on the parents to try to give this child a combination of normal expectations along with a realistic recognition of limitations. If this child is quite capable mentally and only somewhat limited physically, they still will experience a huge challenge in a world that does not tolerate differences very well. If the parents do not create a healthy place for this child by recognizing the limitations but also not putting undue focus on them, it will greatly add to the difficulty for this child. If she/he becomes the main focus in the family, is babied too much, or if no one is realistic about the handicap and pretends it is not there, it can create sibling jealousy and scapegoating.

More importantly, it can, for example, in the case of a little person (dwarf), create massive denial in the child, setting up unrealistic life expectations. I have known such a person, Ruth, who was totally unprepared for puberty or adulthood, because the issue of being a dwarf was not addressed or dealt with by the parents. This implied that this child could have a normal life in a world of taller people, while making her the scapegoat and giving her covert messages that she did not measure up. She lost her mother at a critical time, when she was a teenager beginning to bear the brunt of being shunned for her size. Her father remarried, creating a blended family of two sets of teenagers, all normal in size except for her. The result of this has been severe low self-esteem and an inability to function fully, as an adult. In addition, she suffered many problems with her own addiction, growing up in an alcoholic family. She was not made aware as a child of other little people, so she grew up expecting to have the same experiences as taller people and was therefore unprepared for prejudice, dating, finding a career, and really all areas of her life. She became the scapegoat in her family, with her older sister in the hero role. This brought her to the focus position in a negative way, made her the problem rather than the parents' alcoholism and blended family issues. With her unflagging spirit and very bright mind, she is overcoming the handicap of being the negative focus, which hurt her much more than the physical handicap of being small, and is finding herself and her path.

I also have worked with individuals where there is unresolved pain resulting from a suicide in the family. This traumatic form of death/loss leaves major scars on the family members and affects their relationships. It is often hidden, like a secret that everyone knows about but doesn't talk about, and sometimes is not acknowledged publicly as suicide. This is because the family feels shame about it and somehow feels at fault. If there have been several suicides going down through generations, it usually means that there is a generational theme of people not talking about their problems or painful emotions. Therefore, unable to get out of their pain, they choose death as the only way out. Somewhere along the line, if the family doesn't sit down to grieve and talk about this, or get professional help, the theme will continue. There may be an additional message of shame if the family belongs to a religion in which suicide is considered a sin, rather than a moment of unfathomable mental pain, where one sees no other way out from his/her own repertoire of believed alternatives for relief.

One of the most emotionally harmful themes in a family is that of keeping secrets. Secrets always imply shame and are unhealthy, except when one is planning a happy surprise for someone. Children always know when there are secrets and will form private logic (make things up and figure out as best a child can) to deal with feelings and fears surrounding the issue of secrets. As a theme, this teaches a child to be secretive but not about what specifically, and, therefore, the child grows up being secretive about many things, having used private logic, unable to distinguish what should be in confidence, and is not open in many cases where openness is needed to have healthy relationships. Also, if the child learns what the secret is, and it is about, married cousin Jim having an affair with Aunt Filene, for example, there is a real sexual shame overtone, which the child is too young to digest in perspective to Self and to the adult world.

In another case, if the secret pertains to Dad's mother's suicide for example, it is clear that Dad still carries shame about this, and now his child will, too. Many times the secret is not really a secret per se, but what was long ago coined by literature on alcoholic family themes as, "the elephant in the living room." In this case, everyone in the family knows what the secret is, but it is not talked about, and there is a pretense that it does not exist. This is a form of "crazy making." This was the case with the little person I spoke about earlier. The family acted as if she were normal height. Therefore, she would not use the secret word, "dwarf," in her first year of therapy. I once heard a story about a child asking why Dad was sprawled in the yard, obviously passed out from alcohol, and the mother answered, "Your father is just taking a nap." Secrets and "crazy making" create fear in a child and a feeling of not being safe. As human beings, we crave predictability — not unknowns and surprises. Secrets create barriers in relationships and greatly damage trust. Trust is the most important ingredient needed for forming any relationship and certainly to achieve intimacy.

Another dysfunctional and very hurtful theme that fits right in with secrets, is that of gossip. This can be seen as anything from idle chatter to heavy behind-the-back verbal abuse. However, talking about someone who is not there in any other way than with positive motives of true concern or planning a happy event for them, is gossip. If you want to criticize someone, this needs to be addressed face to face. I always include gossip in workshops that I conduct on verbal abuse and criticism.

In a family where there is gossip, as one of the forms of communication, children learn not to trust people. If Mother talks that way to me about my brother, for example, what does she say to him about me? In my family, there was a full theme of telling negative things to one family member about another. Then, that family member would tell the one talked about what had been said, with their interpretation, for further complication. The family member, who was the object of this round-robin conversation, is hurt or angry and afraid to confront the original gossiper, because the middle party will get in trouble with the gossiper. Of course, the middle party has now become a gossiper, too.

The worst fallout for me was that this kind of behavior, particularly on my mother's part, created terrible rifts and distrusts in my relationship with my sister, which it has taken us years to heal. My sister was eight years younger than me, more compliant as a child, and was Mother's confidant, so the negative stories my mother constantly told her about me largely formed her opinion of me. By being our mother's confidant in this way, along with being privy to our father's alcoholic binges (which I was not), was largely how my sister could have a closer relationship with my mother, while avoiding most of the verbal abuse I suffered as a child. In other words, our sister relationship got sacrificed in this deadly theme of family gossip. We also witnessed our mother gossiping about relatives in very negative ways and then treating them as if they were really special to her. Having personally witnessed this behavior in my mother's and father's family of origins, I have no doubt that this theme was a learned behavior.

Manipulative communication is another theme that is usually handed down for generations. This consists mainly of parents or other caregivers saying one thing and meaning another. This, along with family gossip and outright denial of commitments not kept, creates a lot of "crazy making." "Crazy making" creates all sorts of fallout for children. It leaves them trying to figure out things that truly don't make sense. Children, especially the younger they are, take things literally. When parents communicate with manipulation, the child is left confused and often hurt. One of the most commonly known examples of manipulative communication is where the parent plays the victim and says, "It's okay for you to go out," but the tone or facial expression says, "You are hurting me if you go." The child learns eventually to believe the underlying non-verbal messages, rather than the spoken words. He/she adapts to this form of communication, while also adapting to being controlled by the parents' needs that they are not up front about, and that puts the child in the parent role.

This form of communication often can be the major style in the household. Many comedy routines have been done about manipulative communication, especially many of them about mothers who play a martyr/victim role. When the child grows up, he/she may either adopt this same incongruent (words, tone, and body language don't match) form of communication or always look for hidden meanings in adult communication, therefore, never trusting anyone just on their word. This is by far one of the most common and destructive fallouts that people encounter in couple-ships, as they end up trying to reinterpret what their partner says (figure out the real meaning), because they learned to double guess their parents as a child. In my own healing from this theme in my household, I had to learn to accept people on their word, whether it felt scary to me or not. I always was afraid of misreading the real message and upsetting someone, having been conditioned this way in my family of origin.

Parent-child role reversal is another common theme in many families, where the parents have not had their needs met in their childhood. I often see this theme with mother-daughter relationships in the most obvious ways. My mother did this with myself and my sister. As I mentioned, my mother never received real mothering, being abandoned so young and in so many ways. I also have seen many cases where both parents really were behaving like the children in the family, thus leaving their children to try to take on the caretaker roles.

In Maude's family, with fourteen children, Mom was basically unavailable for anything other than birthing more and more babies and trying to orchestrate meals and laundry. She also had periodic alcoholic binges and would rage out of control, frightening the children. Dad was gone most of the time, working. Child care therefore was allocated to the older children, often in extremely unreasonable amounts, which did not allow time for them to experience childhood. Some of them also were chosen by Dad as go-betweens when mom was drinking, thus putting that child in a little wife role. In terms of guidance, teaching, and parenting, these children were left on their own to survive with their private logic and from the pranks they pulled on each other. Children of alcoholics often grow up in some of these conditions regardless of the number of children. They have to survive unpredictable, emotionally immature, unavailable parents.

Where there is role reversal, it can be all of the children or just one child in particular trying to take care of the parent(s). More often than not, this role reversal falls on the oldest child, who, if there are younger siblings, becomes the little mother or perhaps the little dad. Many times, the surrogate dad/husband can fall to a son, when the father is totally absent or just gone a lot and emotionally unavailable. The same can happen to a daughter where there is no mother in the home because of death, divorce, or career. This child will grow up having lost most of his/her childhood, feeling they always have been an adult. One girl's experience of mother-daughter role reversal also had happened to her mother and to her mother's mother.

In the case of Denise, she took on this role at a very young age when her mother was overwhelmed with her husband's womanizing, the subsequent divorce, and then a series of moves and illnesses that often hospitalized her mom. Denise grew up enmeshed in her mother's pain, feeling she needed to care for her, wanting to make up for her losses, and fearing her mother would die. In addition, Denise was ignored by her father yet expected to be helper and babysitter for his second wife and their children.

As a result, Denise grew up with intense issues of needing to be special, having never felt chosen and never allowed to really be a child. This is one of the main themes from whence we get the term adult child. Adult children of alcoholics actually got that label from themes in an alcoholic family, which usually include role reversals and being thrown into adult roles long before they have grown up. Of course, there are a lot of other inequities in being an adult child, such as the fact that the actual parents do still have the status and power over the children yet expect them to do adult things, but without the privileges that go along with being a grownup. This is another form of "crazy making."

One of the most important factors in healthy family functioning is whether the family has an open or closed system. This determines whether there is air flowing into the system, so to speak, meaning that the system is open and flowing with the outside world and open to new ideas and expression. In a closed system, essentially only the parents (or custodial caregivers) have the answers and want to determine and mold the children to how they believe. There is no room for new ideas or for a child to learn some of his/her lessons by trial and error, without severe and shaming repercussions.

Religiosity is a very good example of a closed system. It is very different from spirituality, which is an open system. When religiosity is a theme in a family, it greatly impacts children, as it can only function in a closed system. It is a theme where religion is the central focus in a rigid, inflexible system of beliefs. It perpetrates fear of God, creates isolation in children by separating them from others as better than, or different. There are rigid black-and-white beliefs about good and bad, right and wrong, and a promised retribution from God. It is inherently shaming. The children are therefore very restricted from emotional and mental growth, which includes exploring, thinking, and verbalizing anything outside of the family's rigid belief system. The children automatically learn to be prejudiced and opinionated in this family system. There is only one way to think or believe. Therefore, others who believe differently are wrong. In these families, the theme of religiosity usually has been present for two or more generations. The impact of a closed system will greatly affect the child's relationship with Self, with family, with God, or higher power, and with every relationship in life. (I will discuss this more fully in Chapter 8: Relationship with Religion and Spirituality.)

Status seeking or looking good are major themes in the American society. When it is a theme in the family, it is always dysfunctional. It is not synonymous with doing your best, or growing into reaching your dreams or potential. Looking good, as a theme in the family, means what is outside and shows is what counts. It is an automatic prescription for a lot of pretending on the outside, shutting out being real, and falling into behavioral patterns to hopefully impress others, giving them the impression that everything is perfect. It is generally about money, things one acquires, power, and status at whatever level the family can achieve, even if all it means is showing up at an important public event in fine clothes and behaving in a picture-perfect way. Meanwhile, at home there may be out-of-control alcoholism, not enough money for necessities, and parents fighting and verbally abusing their children. In some families where there really is plenty of money and power, this may be the major theme of dysfunction. One or both of the parents may have grown up poor, achieved wealth and monetary success, and be driven to perfection, especially in their children.

Perfectionism, which usually is part of a looking-good family theme, is one of the most difficult wounds to heal. These are the dads who "walked ten miles barefoot to school in the snow," to use a metaphor for an often-heard story clients have shared that they were told by a parent to motivate them by shaming. Often a child cannot live up to such standards set by a parent who claims untold hardship, is self-made, and has no understanding that the child is not him or her, and comes from a different life experience and individuality. In some cases, perfectionism exists because the parent feels so personally inadequate that he or she must have a perfect child to display as their claim to achievement. Perfectionism is about wanting a child to live up to the parent's expectations and needs, rather than those of the child. This, like all of the dysfunctional themes, creates distance instead of closeness in relationship. The parent becomes a kind of enemy to avoid or someone to please, rather than a friend and a guide in the development of one's potential.

Some of the dysfunctional themes do, at least, teach ways of relating and connecting, even though they may not be healthy or lasting. The theme of isolation in the family teaches almost nothing about connecting. Isolated families come in several styles. One style is where the family lives in a more isolated environment, like a farm miles from other homes or town, and there is very little opportunity to connect outside the family. If the family is also of a stoic type, where there is little outward emotion or displays of affection, children in this family will learn almost nothing about connecting in relationship. Another style is the family who is comprised of several people, who sort of live in their own worlds, like separate islands. I have known a woman who could hardly tell me anything about her brother, who was only two years younger and the only other child in the family. The parents did not connect in any open ways in the family, so each child likewise learned to live their life in their own isolated space. Fallout for both children, of course, was total lack of knowing how to connect with people, much less in any meaningful or close way.

Finally, there is the enmeshed family, where the family is entangled with each other, even as adults. There are no boundaries, and no one is emotionally allowed to leave home. This can be experienced as a kind of suffocation, where the grownup child may be afraid to connect, because he/she still emotionally is carrying the whole family of origin and/or doesn't know how to connect in relationship without suffocation. I have seen many couples unable to move on with their lives because of their enmeshment with their family of origin and inability to decathect and be free to make their own adult life and connections in a healthy way. One couple with whom I have worked were still enmeshed with their family of origins. Both were afraid to displease their mothers, who held the power in the family of origins, because there was history of emotional and/or complete abandonment by these mothers when they did not like what was going on in the family. Both mothers, each in her own way, tried to control the marriage and expected to be chosen over the spouse. Both people had experienced so much emotional abandonment as children from these mothers that they were still stuck in a deep fear level, rendering them unable to totally commit to each other. To make it worse, both strongly disliked the other one's mother, and it was as if these mothers lived in the house with them, because the arguments and struggles about them dominated so much of their relationship. This, of course, served to continually push them away from intimacy with each other. It often can create a fear of intimacy, as it is seen as being smothered.

Boundaries are a really important issue for us as individuals and especially in our relationships. Parents or caregivers usually have poor boundaries in dysfunctional families. The children do not learn that they are entitled to have their own boundaries, how to create them for themselves, or how to make them in reference to other people. Thus, lack of healthy boundaries is usually a generational theme in many families.

Certainly the enmeshed family is a major example of lack of boundaries. Parents or caregivers will be overly involved with children long after they are grown, not respecting their marriages nor their personal privacy, and sometimes even partially dependent on them. Examples of enmeshed families are where there is too much involvement on an on-going basis. The daughter may be calling Mom every day, even though she needs to take care of her own family. It becomes an obligation to spend all or part of weekends with family of origin, or to visit them on all vacations if living far away, thus eliminating the ability to plan new and interesting things that one's own family might choose. There is expectation to share all things with parents, even though these are private matters that belong only in their nuclear family. Loyalty to family of origin is expected to outweigh loyalty to one's own family. Relationships are, to varying degrees, based on obligation, often with much resentment, rather than based on choice and enjoyment of each other. Though now a grownup, choices of homes, cars, clothing, and general decision making may still have to be checked out with parents, as one is still unsure of Self and still seeking parental approval. We love our parents and always want a relationship with them, so this can be a terribly painful dilemma, especially when there has been a theme of parents' needs superseding the children's needs, going back to childhood. This never-resolved enmeshment leaves the grownup children with unmet needs from childhood and still feeling the obligation to take care of the parents. Sadly, this enmeshment will be repeated again in the next generation with their children.

Setting boundaries within the family is very difficult when the parents have grown up in families with poor boundaries. Children may learn that parents can easily be manipulated out of decisions, partly because the parents are inconsistent and partly because they may parent out of anger, yelling, and setting punishments too severe because they are angry. Then they feel guilty, can be manipulated, and punishment eliminated. Or, the parents are not disciplined themselves and do not want to endure the consequence of staying home themselves, because the child has been grounded and must be supervised. Thus, children grow up, believing boundaries, like rules, can always be manipulated.

We do not feel safe in the world, without good boundaries, because we are not realistically learning what to expect in the world outside. Setting boundaries, with consequences for their violation, teaches us that there are consequences for our behavior. Children, who do not learn this, grow up with many sad, unexpected consequences, such as losing a job, because the boss meant it when he said, "If you continue to be late, you will be fired," or "If you miss work, you will not be paid or not promoted." Also growing up without boundaries means we violate others' boundaries and can suffer rejection and/or humiliation in relationships from those who naturally don't want their boundaries violated. Growing up with poor boundaries will result in:

- Having a poorly defined self.
- Having difficulty knowing where you end and begin.
- Being unaware when you are violating someone else's boundaries.
- Becoming enmeshed with a partner or other important relationships, thus tending to argue or fight your way out.
- Having difficulty enforcing consequences, such as sticking to your guns.
- Being easily manipulated to change your position or tending to be inflexible.
- Never feeling really safe.

Cutting people off is one of the most painful dysfunctional themes that I know. This is a major style of behaviour in dysfunctional families. For many people, such as myself, this is a theme we have seen for generations in our families, where people lacked skills to set boundaries, especially to resolve arguments and hurts. I have seen family members cut off relatives, sometimes ones to whom they were very close, for years at a time, when there is an argument or some hurt that they cannot seem to address with each other. Here, a relationship that was close yesterday seems to no longer exist. These cut-offs are experienced like little deaths. It is a major form of abandonment of Self and of the other person. There has been no closure, so that whatever issue precipitated this is left hanging, added to the collage of painful baggage one already carries inside. Using silence is an emotional cut-off, and the recipient feels like a very high concrete wall has been built that they don't know how to climb. It is extremely punishing, and there is no resolution of the problem, because neither party will break the silence or make an overture, or because one of the parties is unwilling to revisit the issue.

Cutting off is also another breach of trust. It gives the implication, through silence that "you are dead to me." How terrifying for a small child, who is cut off emotionally by a parent with no explanation. This is always experienced as a punishment, which does not fit the crime. When used on children it is very damaging to trust, frightening, and manipulative. It teaches one to tread lightly, and to be apologetic for things that do not really belong to the child. If one has been cut off in a very important relationship, such as from Mom or Dad, and given the silent treatment with no explanation, it will become a major way in which the adult child can later be manipulated in relationships. This is due to the fear of losing the relationship. This will play out in other relationships by being repeated by and upon the recipient. As a child, being cut off emotionally by my mother when she was angry left me with major abandonment issues in my adulthood.

Today, we have a therapeutic intervention method to avoid cut-offs, which I encourage my clients to use when they are locked in a toxic relationship. This means that they can't seem to move past anger and old hurts with someone and tend to get in circular arguments with no resolution. Or, there is just inability to connect and to communicate without getting into anger and/or hurt. This intervention is called a detachment, and can be done as an agreement between two people, or can be done by one party to another who is not actually participating in the decision, to take a time-out. A detachment is different from a cut-off, because it is not done as an angry retaliation but rather as a planned time-out, which is explained (usually by letter) and has boundaries. This means the party receiving the detachment letter is clear that there will be a re-connection, when it will be, and is not blamed for the detachment. It is important to remember that when we are angry at people who we love, we will always want or wish for connection with them, except in very extreme cases of abuse. Often, we cannot feel the love when angry or hurt, but the very fact that we hold onto the anger so desperately and often obsess about it is pure implication of how important these relationships are to us.

The need we have to be connected to those we care about is major, so we need closure to issues that block connection. They are relationships, especially family of origin, who comprise integral parts of our psyche. We are driven to try to resolve them, often through many incidences of transference in our lifetime. Cut-offs, or putting it in the past, don't resolve anything, and just leave us with symptoms of the unresolved toxicity, which we continue to play out in other relationships. Detachment allows us to get out of the toxic trap and to find more of ourselves. After all, we can only change ourselves — what a bummer! Many a relationship has greatly improved only because one party took the time-out to look at Self and find out what their part had been in the toxic relationship. Usually, it involves always trying to control/change the other person! This improvement can occur, even though the other party has their half part of the dysfunction in the relationship and may not have changed at all. When there is sincere Self-searching and willingness to change on your part, it doesn't even matter as much sometimes that the other person didn't change, or "own their stuff."

As you can see, our family of origin is woven into the fabric of our being through the complexities of relationship. It is believed by many, myself included, that we become our parents to a large degree. Actually, in many ways we become our entire family of origin, even including our ancestors. In the quest to become healthy and have healthy, well-functioning relationships, it is infinitely useful to learn all we can about our immediate family and their ancestors. In investigating our family, we inevitably will see patterns and scenes unfold like a finely connected tapestry. There can be people, who are/were colorful, events, and struggles that were somewhat disastrous or highly successful, and painful scenes of darker color. But, most of all, these themes and patterns will unfold and will show you where you came from, what characteristics have been passed down generationally, how relationships have worked — or not worked — and why, and how all this connects to who you are and where you are today. Even if your search brings pain and a look at a history that you feel shame about, you will find that seeing it before you is healing, as it allows you to now choose a different path. It is often said that families are comprised of good people who do the best they can in most cases. This is true, but the other truth is that what they do has an impact — which is what this book is about — and we can only function differently by honestly and openly looking at and healing those impacts that wounded us.

Note: Questions relating to this chapter are at the end of Chapter 4.

Chapter Four

RELATIONSHIP WITH FAMILY OF ORIGIN

Will have the most profound effects on our choices and behaviors

These are some of the most profound issues and behaviours by caretakers that have affected us most deeply in dysfunctional families. If there is a theme of gender preference, sexual and/ or verbal abuse in your family stew, then your Self will be most deeply impacted.

Gender preference is another family theme that will create low self-esteem in a family, such as a preference for boys over girls. Children know this whether it is clearly verbalized or not. Historically, there has been a theme of male preference. Dads want sons — or are believed to want sons — more than daughters. Mothers also hope for a son, so that the husband will be happy and to express things that her role cannot. Unfortunately, sometimes a son of a divorced mother feels a male bias in his mom. In some countries, this desire for boys over girls is tragic, such as in China, where there are still some female babies being killed, especially if the parents are allowed only one child. Though America is not known for that, it can still cause great hurt and self-esteem problems for girls, who know their parents, would have preferred a boy. Also, for the boy in a family where he holds such importance, the parenting will very much favor him, ensuring he gets the best education, etc., whereas the girl(s) will not be treated with such importance. This gender preference has seen many a girl try to become "daddy's boy." My sister did this for a few years, sacrificing some or much of her sexual identity to gain Dad's favor and trying to fill our parents' needs rather than her own.

As I mentioned in my introduction, our founding fathers brought many dysfunctional themes with them to this country. Preference for male children was one of them. This also can put a very large burden on the "boy child," which he may not be able or want to live up to. Sometimes there is so much male preference in one generation that daughters grow up almost hating men. Then, her son(s), and often other men in her life, will pay for what she experienced, because she will not like them, having had so much jealousy of her brothers.

In a gender-prejudiced family, and in other families, too, there is too often homophobia. Where this is the case, the gay, lesbian, bisexual, and/or other sex-oriented child will suffer great humiliation and will be very shame-based in going off to school and out in the world, where more humiliation will be added. In these families the homosexually oriented child will have no hope of meeting parents' expectations. In fact, the sexual orientation can and usually will block out other achievements. In many cases, this child is disowned or ignored and really starves for affection and approval. Ignoring the child's sexual orientation or rejecting it is felt in the Self of the child. This very often creates a whole secret life, splitting Self into two selves, one presented in the outside world of heterosexuals and the other who leads a secret life of homosexuality. This problem is what creates a subculture of dysfunction. Here gather many of them who are angry, full of dislike of Self, acting out in extremes in unhealthy ways. The outside world then sees this as representing the gay lifestyle, and it reinforces prejudice. Many people with alternate sexual lifestyles choose to be in the closet, not wishing to be part of this kind of subculture and endure increased prejudice.

Gender prejudice coming down through history is how we have ended up with patriarchal families, where men have the most power, and matriarchal families, where women have predominance of power. All of these gender prejudices create gender themes that deeply affect the child's self-esteem, modes of adapting in the family, ability to be a successful adult, and ability to function in relationship, especially with the opposite sex or same sex in partnership. We see an example of gender preference in the movie, The Color Purple, where Sophie and her aunts have formed a powerful, female defense against men in the family, who it is implied, are sexual predators. There also can be a severe impact on personal sexual identity.

VERBAL AND/OR PHYSICAL ABUSE

Physical and/or sexual abuse can and too often is a dysfunctional theme in the family. Today, for the most part in our country, the trend is to avoid physical punishment. This includes any kind of hitting or touching a child in a hurtful or angry manner. I am actually confounded by those who still want to hold onto any version of the old saying, "Spare the rod and spoil the child." First, we only spoil a child by substituting things for love and by not setting boundaries. Second, if a parent is an emotionally healthy adult, loves his/her child, knows how to and is willing to set boundaries and non-physical consequences for inappropriate or unacceptable behaviors, there is never need for hitting and/or verbal abuse. Children need and want boundaries. While we are growing up, we feel safe and secure when we know what the boundaries are in our home. This prepares us to function within boundaries set by others. Parents hit children generally out of their own fear or in anger, as if expecting the child to know everything and/or be perfect, or because they are immature themselves. In some cases, they are just too impatient to endure the consequences they may have to endure themselves, such as grounding the child, or not allowing television, computer, or video games for a period of time.

When the child is first born up to about ages two or three, parents need to childproof their home, be kind and loving (yet firm) while speaking to the toddler about his/her behavior(s), using distractions rather than always saying no, and be very, very present and patient. Hitting a child, who is only a toddler and cannot comprehend or connect it to learning, only will teach him/her to hit others and deeply damage self-esteem. As the child gets a little bigger, there can be time-outs, and other non-abusive consequences can begin to be set. Making clear what the rules and consequences are for breaking them and following through will make a child feel secure while not damaging his/her self-esteem. This kind of parenting addresses only the behaviors, whereas, hitting or cutting off gives the message that the child is bad.

Many of us have been hit, had hair pulled, fingernails dug in the arm, kicked (and more) by parents, who were mistreated in the same ways by their parents. The fallout is on our self-esteem. This creates internal wounds of hurt and anger, teaching us that hitting is okay and that we are bad.

Sexual abuse is a very sad and complicated issue. It is a kind of abuse that affects us to the core of our being. We cannot separate our sexuality from who we are. It is a major part of how we become who we are, and it is core to our continuing existence and our ability to make the most intimate connection possible. Thus, sexual abuse and incest leave permanent scars. They affect how we view sexuality, how we are able to be sexual (or not), and most of all how we feel about Self, as we are left burdened with sexual shame. Today, we know that the appeal of pornography and prostitution are fallout for one's being inappropriately energized sexually. This sexual energizing is then a psychological trigger from the brain for the body to become energized in whatever way it originally was energized. This, of course, greatly interferes with heart intimacy, as the sex drive is connected only to sexual objectifying, not to a love interest. The heart and the genitals have become separated. The best example of this is when a parent or other important adult in the child's life commits incest. This violates the child's core boundaries, and confuses and scares the child about parental safety and boundaries.

Our country is still struggling about accepting alternative sexual orientations, which are known to be much more varied than was realized before. Basically the issue of some religious beliefs is the greatest block to giving equal rights to these individuals. It seems strange that our country of freedom is more resistant and often abusive than other countries on this subject of gay, lesbian, transsexual, bisexual, etc. Thus, many fine people suffer for their sexual orientation and the right to have it.

Verbal abuse experienced during childhood creates negative beliefs about Self, which we continue to repeat to ourselves forever, unless we actively work to change these beliefs. These ingested beliefs destroy one's self-esteem. I believe that most families use a great deal of verbal abuse. This includes any one or all of the following:

- Direct character assassinating, such as, "You are an idiot."
- Indirect negative messages, such as, "I'll just do it myself." Or, "You aren't going to wear that blouse you have on with those slacks, are you?"

- Silent messages, being cut off, or the look that says, "You are not in my favor," all of which you interpret to mean you are bad.
- Gossip in the family about people in the family.
- Sarcasm, which is a way of saying something that is derogatory to someone, using anger cloaked in humor, so that the one who says it does not have to take responsibility for the dig.
- Criticism

Dysfunctional families are loaded with these types of critical, verbally abusive communication. In my, family my mother showered me with criticism on a daily basis. I never remember being affirmed by her as a child for anything. Everything I did, said, wore, accomplished, wanted, or tried, seemed to meet with her disapproval. I was her personal scapegoat, with any problems in the family being my fault. Ultimately, this included my father's alcoholism and his early death. Though I was, from age thirteen on, very popular, very successful in academics, athletics, and extracurricular activities, nothing could fill the need I had inside for my mother's approval. Though I didn't know what was wrong at that time, I thought I had won by getting her attention through rebellion. I now know I was suffering from that core, unmet need of all children. And, that need is to be loved, chosen, and approved of by a parent.

For a girl, I believe this is especially true in her relationship with her mother. The result of all of my mother's verbal abuse left me hating myself, as a young girl. Later, as a parent, I verbally abused my own children, and for years have remained unfairly critical of myself.

Probably the greatest emotional damage I have seen from verbal abuse was carried by a man named Gil. When I met him, he was tortured inside with shame, anger, self-doubt, and an immense fear of people. He was the second-born child but surrounded by three sisters, who, along with his mother (who clearly and deeply

Anne Salter, LCSW

disliked males), gave him daily and on-going tirades of verbal abuse. He was a sweet child and longed for the love and approval of his mother, and tried hard to please her. His father had a career in the Army, was often not home, was totally uninvolved with parenting, was submissive to Gil's mother, and there were no father-son activities. Gil was left entirely at the mercy of his three sisters' teasing and his mother's rages, which he described as very scary and out of control. Gil became the scapegoat and was blamed for fights or arguments with the girls. He was told he was a "Mongolian idiot," "stupid," "retarded," and that he would never amount to anything. His mother and sisters would trick and betray him. Gil remembers the toxic teasing being endless, and he withdrew more and more to a secret life.

As an army family, they moved often, including overseas, and he had to frequently adjust to new schools and to new people. He entered these situations with very low self-esteem and intense fear. Despite this negative input, he amazingly was able to become a Marine pilot and later an airline pilot. But, in his personal life he was constantly depressed. It took an incredible amount of losses for him in his personal life, including a failed marriage, a ruined career, and financial challenges, for him to surrender to his co-dependency and to his addiction illness, which had been created almost entirely out of verbal abuse. He still struggles with the co-dependent behaviors. Though he has made immense progress through diligent work and therapy, he still fears that he innocently will offend someone, who will then shame him.

As you can see, I wholeheartedly believe that verbal abuse permeates the very core of our being. And, that we experience it not only in the ways I have just named, but also in the messages of devaluation we receive or have interpreted from any physical and/or sexual abuse we have experienced.

Before we move on to specific focus on how we have been affected by family of origin, start your self study with the questionnaire at the end of this chapter and remember to share it with your therapist.

QUESTIONNAIRE ON RELATIONSHIP WITH FAMILY OF ORIGIN

1. Name the people in the family that you grew up with: mother, father, sisters, brothers, stepparents, other caregivers, such as grandparents, or other relatives that you knew well, or who played a major role in your childhood.
1. Write a brief sentence or two describing each of these people who are immediate family and/or played a major role in your childhood. Describe your relationship with each of them.
2. Are you aware of any childhood decisions that you made in reaction to people or events in your family? How about self-fulfilling prophesies?
3. Were there healthy boundaries in your family of origin? Write about this.
4. Did your family use cutting off to deal with anger and/or hurt? Describe.
5. Was there chronic illness, a handicapped family member, or other factor that consumed most of the family's focus and resources? If yes, write about it and how it affected you.
6. Was there abuse in your home? Physical? Sexual? Verbal? (include sarcasm)
7. Which of the following themes were part of your family dynamics and how did you experience them? Write all you know about the ones that apply to you:

   Addiction (see and answer questions in Chapter 16)
   Status seeking/looking good
   Isolation
   Manipulative communication
   Gender preferences/prejudice
   Religiosity
   Parent-child role reversals

Shame
Anger
Abandonment
Perfectionism
Enmeshment

8. Was your family a closed or open system?
9. Were you or are you still enmeshed with family of origin?
10. Begin writing your life story. (You will add to it as you read this book.)

CHAPTER FIVE

RELATIONSHIP WITH GRANDPARENTS, RELATIVES AND CARETAKERS

Were there angels in your life?

O ur relationships with our early caretakers are very important. Grandparents and other relatives with whom we have had a good amount of contact are especially meaningful. Even if we did not know them or rarely saw them, they bring to us not only their particular style of connecting, but also the history of their parenting of our parents, along with their origins. Knowing their history and origins can bring us additional awareness. Besides their family history, we get their cultural origins. From this, we can learn about many of our behaviors and beliefs, which are culturally handed down. When we do not have this connection to our history, it is what I call a missing piece, regarding our identity. We lack a fuller sense of knowing who we are. For example, knowing that I am Scottish-Irish-German can explain in many ways some of the behaviors and traditions in my family. There are stereotypes of ethnic groups, but there is some truth in many of them. For example, Germans tend to be more stern and stoic. This fits for my mother's family. Irish have a strong history of excessive drinking of alcohol and of religious fundamentalism. This fits for my family, too, especially on the paternal side. The excessive relationship with alcohol fits on both sides of my family. I learned all of this, from where my ancestors originated and in the history telling of an older family member, along with my own experience.

In some cases, a grandparent or a special aunt or uncle can be an important key to how we survived dysfunctional parenting and themes in our nuclear family. On the other hand, if these relatives are part of a large, enmeshed family, it often can mean more conflicting messages, more confusion, and witnessing of unresolved issues between the parent and grandparent, aunt or uncle. In addition to this, the relationship modeling teaches the child that no one ever leaves the family of origin. It can feel like an unfathomable trap and cause untold problems when one grows up and begins their nuclear family, only to find it loaded with our parents' unresolved family-of-origin relationships.

Additional adult caretakers in our childhood can sometimes be like angels in our lives, someone who gave us love and attention and was affirming and uncritical of our Self. Even if this relationship only lasted a short time, especially in early childhood, it can leave a lasting, positive impact on self-esteem. Also, this relationship with a grandparent, for example, is often very different from the relationship this grandparent had as the parent of one of our own parents. Certainly, my children's relationships with their grandmothers was far more positive than had been mine or my husband's in our growing up with them as parents.

Many children are raised by a grandparent, and that can be positive or negative. If this grandparent has mellowed and grown since raising his/her own children (our parents), then it can be positive. However, it can be very hurtful if the grandparent(s) bad-mouths the parent who is absent. Making comments, such as "You are just like your lazy mother/father," can have a very negative impact on self-esteem. Unfortunately, and especially after a divorce, this kind of negative commenting also goes on far too often by one parent about the other. In some of the most difficult and abusive childhoods, many times I have seen a special relative (sometimes an aunt), who has basically saved a child emotionally. It was the person with whom the child could trust his/her sharing of the most personal feelings, thoughts, and fears. It was a safe harbor to run to when the immediate family was in chaos or violence was occurring. This experience with an aunt or uncle being so much safer can leave the child wishing this relative was their real mom or dad. This often breeds confusion and guilt in the child.

Jim had a nanny from early childhood, who was his closest and most stable relationship. His father was an airline pilot, who traveled frequently and was often gone for three-month periods. His mother was very young, on the go a lot, and sometimes traveled with his father for a few months. Though he was clearly his mother's favorite of the three boys, he still experienced emotional abandonments when his mother was gone. He loved his nanny, and long since as an adult, he would visit her to make sure she was comfortable, even though she lived in a foreign country. She was a loving and dependable caretaker. When he was eleven, he was sent off to boarding school, something that was often done in well-to-do families in his country. Though he thought he wanted this, it turned out to have a powerful, negative impact in his emotional development and self-esteem. At his age, it was a frightening place to be. He missed his parents, especially his mother. However, it was not acceptable culturally for him to ask to go home. This only increased his longing for his mother, and, as an adult, he could not do enough for her or buy her enough gifts, though she never asked for anything. It was his continuing need to feel special to his mother and probably his very young inner child's need to be sure he wasn't abandoned, though this was not a real threat for him as an adult. (Our wounded child sometimes causes behaviors that are compulsions coming from a very young part of Self). However, without his nanny, he would have experienced much more abandonment. She was an angel in his life.

A grandfather or an uncle can be a strong and important fill-in for a missing parent, such as a dad. Of course, sadly, sometimes a grandparent or other relative can turn out to be an abuser or a sexual perpetrator. This has much the same effect on the child as if it were a parent. It can cause conflicts between the child and a parent, as the parent may not want to face that his/her mother or father would do this to the child.

There are many old rules that most of us heard while growing up. One of those is about honoring and respecting your elders. This is often "crazy making" if these elders do not practice respectful behaviors themselves.

Sandra did not tell her mother about her grandfather's abuse until she was grown. Her mother still was trying to get her father's approval (unresolved baggage) and found it hard to accept her daughter's claim. Sandra wanted her mother to cut off communication with her father and was very angry when she refused. Now, Sandra had a deep rift not only with her grandfather, but also with her mother. They finally worked it out by doing joint therapy for several months.

Another kind of caretaker or very influential adult in a child's life is his/her teachers. I am grateful that much of the learning arena has changed since I was a child, but especially grateful that more and more teachers are nurturing, patient, and affirming of the children they teach, especially for a child from an abusive home. Whether the abuse is physical, verbal, sexual, or just neglectful, a teacher can have a major impact on this child. Offering special attention and recognizing that this child is unhappy and fear-driven from experiences at home, this teacher can offer a different experience — where the child, who would have given up, does not. I realize this kind of caretaking is very difficult, as schools and teachers are not supported by the system.

Blended families often are very difficult for the parents and the children. There is often resentment among the children about losing one of their biological parents, whether in divorce or death. There are large adjustments to be made in most aspects of their lives, such as where they live, who their neighbors are, with whom they share a room, whether they like their new stepparent. They may perceive that they have lost both parents in the fact that one is not in the home and the other is more attentive to the new spouse. Where there has been death of a parent or divorce where one parent moves away, there is a lot of loss going on for each child, and often no one is attentive to this pain. Forming relationships and sharing with their new brothers and sisters is another whole difficult challenge.

One blended family I have known mistreated and cheated their handicapped child by making her the scapegoat and leaving her out of important events and other special things for the other children. This child had lost her mother to death before her father married another woman. The stepmother favored her own children and displayed a need to have the family look good at all times. She wanted to hide the handicapped child, who looked different from the other siblings. Unfortunately, this child's father went along with this alcoholic stepmother and enabled her to treat the child very unfairly. No matter how hard this child tried to win the stepmother's love, it was to no avail. The stepmother treated her as if she cared about her to her face, but then gossiped about her and left her out of family trips, weddings, and social events where she would be seen. Eventually, this child became alcoholic as a teenager and got into trouble acting out. Her siblings did not help her, especially her own sister, who was Dad's favorite. This young woman is a miracle today, as she has worked so hard on recovery of her self-esteem and from addiction. The family remains the same.

A friend of mine shared that she had grandparents who rescued her, when her mother repeatedly left her in foster homes. They provided a stable household for her during her early years. They also saved her life by getting penicillin for her when she had rheumatic fever. Her home was very abusive, so it seems clear that the interventions of those grandparents helped her to survive.

I have heard many stories of early childhood sexual abuse by babysitters and by neighbors. These incidents are not only hurtful, destroying boundaries and inappropriately energizing the child sexually, but also are very confusing, destroying trust of other people and setting up distorted expectations for the child.

These relationships with our relatives, neighbors, teachers, and babysitters teach us, as children, how to view the world. In dysfunctional families, we learn to adapt in distorted ways, avoid and fear people, yet still depend on these people. No wonder children of these families grow up and give off double messages such as, "I need you, but I don't trust you, and I am afraid of you." No wonder we do not have a fully formed identity or good self-esteem and don't feel prepared for life. Sadly, we usually repeat the beliefs and behaviors that we learned in these relationships, unless we become aware through self-healing.

Questionnaire about Relationships with Grandparents and other Caretakers

1. Write in depth about all of your relationships that fit this category.
2. Did you know any/all of your grandparents? If so, describe them.
3. Describe any other important relatives or caretakers in your life.
4. How did these relationships impact your life? Are you aware of behaviors and/or beliefs that are a result of them?
5. Were there any angels in your life, who helped you survive emotionally?
6. Did you grow up in a blended family? If so, write about your experience.

Chapter Six

RELATIONSHIP WITH SIBLINGS

Can Create Lifelong Baggage

Our sisters and brothers are the most important of our early relationships, second only to our relationships with our parents. Even if we are an only child, we are affected by the lack of siblings, as to what we could have learned and experienced with them, and how our parents treat us differently as an only child. The same is true, by the way, when we are missing a parent. We are denied the important relationship with a father or mother and find ourselves fumbling in choosing, for example, male friends or mates, or female friends or mates. Of course, these missing relationships could have had a positive or negative impact on us, but there is still an impact without them. It is one of those missing pieces in the forming of our identity.

Sisters and/or brothers bring with them a myriad of relationship impacts growing up. I have discussed the adapting of roles by each child in a dysfunctional family and how they interact. Sometimes they are invasive of each other, and sometimes they are isolated from each other, particularly in a family like Mary's, where everyone was in a role, yet each person in the family was isolated. They were like separate islands, and no one got emotional needs met. The parents were alcoholics, who were distant from each other at home, only being together for partying and drinking outside the home. There was no communication of emotional needs, as no parent was available, so they all made their own world. As adults, even though they had the four traditional adaptive roles of hero, scapegoat, lost child, and mascot, they were lost when it came to forming important relationships. They struggled as adults, most being dominated by their partner, as their mother had been, and willing to sacrifice their needs. Mary and Frances were particularly affected in this way and could not stand up for their needs, as they then rationalized about their partners' behaviors and selfishness.

A more common situation that we see, especially in addictive families, is a lot of chaos, parents fighting, children fighting with each other — yet being yelled at for fighting, even though this was what they learned to do in relationship from their parents' behaviors.

This was also the case for the four children in Jerry's family, where everyone was their enemy. This leaves each child in fear, not only of the parents, but also of each other. They function competitively; parents blame each other and compete to be the favorite of each child. The other theme in the family, besides addiction, was about intellectual supremacy and success. Like most children in this situation, these four children strove toward high success, except Jerry, who, as the scapegoat, kept setting himself up to fail and therefore maintained his role in the family. This was what I call a starving family, multi-addicted, including severe eating disorders in both parents, which were later developed by three of the four children. The saddest part is that these children cannot support each other, so in the opposite way from Mary's family, they also were isolated from nurture and starving emotionally. Naturally, they have struggled with relationships as adults, especially more intimate ones. When primary modelling behavior by parents is about fighting, blaming, and abusing, it is, unfortunately, natural for the children to practice these same dysfunctional behaviors when forming their close relationships.

In Brenda's family, with an alcoholic father and a very co-dependent, enabling mother, there were three older brothers. Brenda, quite a bit younger than her brothers, was the baby. As children, the boys were very competitive to be the favorite, and one brother was the designated favorite of mom. However, being mom's favorite did not mean that he was not starved and angry. He expected to inherit more and to be chosen over the others. His brothers, as adults, were very angry, too, withholding from their mother, as no doubt they had felt withheld from, and not wanting to participate in their mom's care as she grew old. Brenda, clearly a hero child, growing up mostly without these brothers around, learned to cope by being extremely busy and running all the time. She developed a kind of love-hate feeling toward her mother but then still took care of her, yearning to be recognized for herself in a special way. No doubt, their anger was not only at their alcoholic, womanizing, physically and verbally abusive father, but also toward Mom for putting up with it, for not leaving, and for subjecting them to his behaviors. Brenda was not close to her brothers because of the age differences, added to the family experiences. In her co-dependent, subservient role, her mother had modeled for Brenda that women were to tolerate men, no matter how abusive they were, and that men were the most important people. Her relationship, not only with her father, but also with these angry distant brothers, saw her grow up having many painful difficulties in relating to men. She had an extremely painful first-love experience, being abandoned, and then four failed marriages, one of which was to an addict. Her son (another male relationship) became an addict, bringing more pain for her in relationship. Her wonderful and very intelligent personality has led her to want to help others, especially her son, though her co-dependency causes her to go overboard. She learned to do tough love with her son and through this experience is starting to find a path to pursue her recovery.

My relationship with my sister has had a major impact on my life. I was an only child for eight years, and though I thought I wanted a baby sister, I was ready to send her back after only a few weeks! Of course, I could not realize the implications of having a sibling, especially with my fear-based mother, who had no clue how to parent, nurture, or be there for a child. What she did was make my sister the favorite, probably because I was such a curious, highly energetic child who fought her at every turn. My sister was much more timid, did not cause waves, and went along with mother's needs. However, after she grew up, she made it a point to live far away from Mother. Though I was my father's favorite, he was elusive and gone most of the time. As we grew up, our mother constantly built wedges between me and my sister, telling her that I was untrustworthy and generally not good.

On the other hand, when my younger sister started high school, my mother would throw my high school successes and popularity in her face, and she never was able to live up to my achievements. This was partly because my sister and I were very different, with different interests, and partly because academics came easily to me. Thus, my sister and I disliked each other, did not bond, and were jealous of each other. It has taken many years for us to heal our relationship through therapy and learning to respect each other's differences. I am glad we have been persistent!!

I shared about a man in Chapter Four, who grew up with tremendous verbal abuse. It was not just his parents who did this, but also his three sisters, who would taunt him, trick him, and make fun of him. The outcome has been, among other problems, a great fear of women. The few times he has chosen to marry or form a committed love relationship have ended in his being betrayed. He longs for a close relationship but is terrified of women. This is a direct result of sibling abuse and no support from mother or father.

Another family I have mentioned, where there were fourteen children, an alcoholic mother and workaholic dad, found the children always in chaos, basically left to raise themselves and each other. Their need for attention became a house full of pranks and tricks on each other, along with incestuous relationships. This was their only way of getting nurture. The fallout has been their having great difficulties in relationship, sex addiction or sexual anorexia, not forming close relationships, dysfunctional marriages, etc. Here we see sibling relationships as critical to survival, yet with a devastating impact because of non-functional parenting.

I also mentioned in another chapter how a sibling can be so important, that the other child or children are almost ignored. I shared about a boy, who tried to become his dead brother to take care of his parents' loss of this very favorite child and, therefore, to become more special to them. This was a great tragedy, as his identity was totally denied and undeveloped.

Another woman I have known, who grew up with three brothers, was a victim of incest by one of them, leaving her very hurt and angry. She was shy in nature and non-confrontational, and she told no one. Her father was known as the town drunk. However, her oldest brother was very safe and nurturing to her, and she was devastated when he left to go into the military, when she was six years old. Her mother was not very available, basically carrying the family, and her other brothers taunted and teased her. She developed an eating disorder in the process of trying to nurture herself and functioned as a lost child. The safety and nurture of the older brother for those first six years of her life probably helped her to survive. On the other hand, her experiences with her other brothers left her with negative feelings about men, and herself.

Jennifer was the superhero in her family of origin. She tried to take care of everyone. For her severely alcoholic mother, she made sure all was in order, dinner made, laundry done, etc., so that when her functional alcoholic father came home from work, there would be no anger and fighting, including beating her mother. As a teenager after her mother had died, Jennifer attended functions with her father, like a little wife. She made sure that this family looked good. She did not criticize nor fight with her two sisters. Outside of the home, she excelled at everything, reflecting achievements and good things on the family. While her sisters also excelled, they played additional dysfunctional roles. One was the scapegoat, the other the lost child. Jennifer grew up being everyone's caretaker. Her needs were not considered. Whether it was a friend, a spouse, her family or whomever, she would drop everything to help them out or rescue them. As years passed, she ended up financially able to help anyone in need. She loaned money, knowing it would not be returned. Eventually, her sister, Marta, lost and/or spent her wealth, was no longer married or working, and had hit an emotional bottom. Jennifer felt it was her job to take care of her financially and emotionally. Fearful that Marta might commit suicide, Jennifer had her move nearby into one of her rental properties, so that she could be there for her twenty-four-seven. The sister was depressed. Jennifer became depressed, saying "When I am with, her I feel angry, and when I am not, I feel guilty." As children, Jennifer was the designated good girl, and Marta was the designated bad girl. Jennifer feels guilt over this, as if she had it better in this very emotionally abusive family, where she had to take care of everything and everyone. Jennifer was terrified to say no to any request and offered more than was asked. This case of extreme co-dependency was destroying them both. They both decided to go for help. The hero child often can be the most difficult to help in therapy, because they are so enmeshed in the role of caretaker, having to know all the answers and in fear of being needy.

As you can see, sibling relationships are very powerful and impacting. Hopefully, you can look at your own and gain insights into how they have influenced your behaviors and choices.

Questionnaire on Relationship with Siblings

1. Did/do you have siblings? How many? Name and describe.
2. How was your relationship with each sibling?
3. How has this affected your adult relationships with men? With women?
4. If you are an only child, how has this affected your adult relationships?
5. What role did you play in your family?
6. What role did each of your siblings play in your family?

Chapter Seven

RELATIONSHIP WITH ANIMALS AND PETS

A Safe Emotional Intimacy

Pets are very dear to so many millions of us in our society. Many people respond positively to animals, especially to dogs, cats and others that are commonly owned as pets. Historically, our relationship and treatment of animals has altered dramatically. Except in certain cultures and religions, where a particular animal has been believed to be sacred, such as the cow in the Hindu religion, animals were seen and used as workers and beasts of burden. In some societies, cats and dogs were/are eaten. The word animal often has been used in a very derogatory fashion, especially in reference to sex practices, referring to our baser nature.

In terms of our relationship to pets, it is often true that though one may grow up in a very dysfunctional and perhaps abusive family, one's relationship with pets is not as impacted as are the relationships (and future ones) with people. One explanation is that often a family pet in a dysfunctional family is a child's only safe relationship. On the other hand, the dog or cat also may be held more dearly by Mom or Dad and treated more lovingly than the children. This often will have a negative impact on a child who feels left out or dis-favored over a dog or cat. This child may grow up doing the same thing as the parent and/or not like pets because of their experience of having a pet favored over them.

One such example of this dysfunctional behavior is a family I know where a mother treats her little dog like a beloved baby, while ignoring her daughter. She comes home from work and cuddles the dog, spending no time with the daughter. The daughter is ignored most of the time, has low self-esteem, and the family wonders why she seems to be angry. Here, a pet has become like a second child, replacing the first one — the real one.

One mother, who wanted to take on the child's role when with her daughter, was very jealous of the daughter's love and attention to her cats. This mother had never had real mothering and, therefore, (unknowingly) had put her daughter in a role-reversal position. Though unable to mother her daughter, she still had a need for the attention her daughter gave the cats. Her need to be mothered was normal, though unrealistic that it could be met in this way.

Many adults who cannot seem to form close and intimate relationships will get dogs or cats, sometimes birds and even an iguana and other more exotic animals, with whom they form a relationship that mimics that animal being their child. Dogs and cats especially accept humans on almost any terms and are content just being a best friend, so they feel very safe to people who have never felt safe with other people. They will put up with the eccentricities of their owners, even if that includes not being well-cared for at times. They are companions for an otherwise isolated existence and do not argue or reject their owner.

This is a very common occurrence with the lost child, who has withdrawn as much as possible from people and is afraid of close relationships. Pets give them companionship and something to love that feels safe. One young man I knew made his dog his higher power, when he was feeling so alone during his recovery. Very lost children are often the ones who collect pets, often have too many, and feel compelled to save as many as possible. I have heard a lost child refer to it as wanting to "save the babies." This is a result of trauma around their childhood, and how unsafe the human babies were in their family.

Collecting, or saving pets is not exclusive to the lost child role. The hero child also will want to "save the babies," because saving the family or a particular member of the family is their theme in this hero role, along with saving people, places, and things. The scapegoat child will view a pet as a rejected being, who like themselves, needs someone to love them. They may, however, treat the pet harshly at times, having been parented that way. In a sense, this is using the pet as a scapegoat. Finally, the mascot child will be needy for a pet's love but inconsistent in the care, because this role is often frenetic. In these adapted roles, there is that underlying need to gain some kind of unconditional love, which they did not get in childhood.

Relationship with animals also can turn out to be very negative and abusive. For example, in a chaotic family where there is a lot of anger and inconsistency in parenting, the pet will become neurotic, sometimes even growling or biting at the owner. This is not the given nature of that pet, but in this case, this pet has become unsure and defensive, much like the rest of the family. It will be nervous and unruly. A pet in a dysfunctional family, where there is a co-dependent head-of-household with no boundaries, will be difficult, if not impossible, to train. Training, like parenting, requires love, boundaries, and consistency.

Another example of negative and abusive attitudes and treatment of animals is that of growing up in abusive families, where animals and children are so abused, that the children grow up only to repeat this behavior onto other helpless and vulnerable animals, just as they, too, had been vulnerable as children.

An example of animal abuse in a family was told by a young man, who said his father had made him watch while he tortured cats. Naturally, this not only gave the message that animals were not valued, but also that this father was capable of inhumane treatment and, therefore, might be capable of doing the same to his son.

Another major example of animal abuse is cock fighting and dog fighting. It reminds one of Roman days when gladiators were trained to fight to the death for others' entertainment. No one growing up in a healthy, non-abusive family would ever participate in such sports, where animals are used to entertain without any regard for the animal's life! Historically, there has been cockfighting in certain cultures, where there also has been less regard for human life.

It has been found that very violent people, like serial killers, often torture and kill animals as practice.

Finally, it is easy to see how our relationship with pets and other animals is another reflection of our childhood learning and experiences. Many of us have heard the parable about how the boss yells at his employee, and then the employee comes home and yells at his mate, the mate yells at their child, and the child kicks the cat. This, is a great example of how we learn from the top down and continue dysfunctional abusive practices, passing them on to the children, who will then grow up to repeat what they have learned.

Questionnaire on Relationship with Animals and Pets

1. Have you/do you own a pet?
2. What is your relationship with animals/pets?
3. What did you experience in your family of origin with/ about pets?
4. Did you ever have a hurtful experience with an animal? If so, did this turn you against animals or specifically that kind of animal.

CHAPTER EIGHT

RELATIONSHIP WITH RELIGION AND SPIRITUALITY

Whose Beliefs Are These? Did I choose them?

C arl Jung, the great psychologist, wrote, "Spirituality is my way of life." I believe it is either healthy or unhealthy, reflected in my thinking, speaking, acting, and in the quality of my relationships. This includes the quality of my relationship with my Self, with others, and with all of life.

In this chapter, I will show how relationship with religion, if it incorporates the dynamics of a dysfunctional family — especially if it is a closed system — can have a very profound effect on the growth and development of a child and, therefore, on adult functioning in relationships, and our relationships with other cultures and countries.

The history of religion, based on research and facts, does not match what is taught in many churches, synagogues, and mosques. This, along with many, many different interpretations of the Bible causes a lot of confusion and "crazy making" for children brought into these denominations by their parents. It also will create fear and shame in a child, who begins to question or reject any of it, as they become more exposed to other ideas and interpretations in school and society. They often will experience alienation and/or confusion at school, because of their rigid beliefs, and having to choose between family, salvation, or making friends and learning more about the world. Sometimes, they learn to hate differences.

Children, because they are the most open at an early age, often have very early experiences with spirituality and/or religion. They are ready to ingest whatever their caretakers put forward and to form their most deeply imbedded belief systems. In fact, they come into the world spiritually connected, ready to love and be loved, with no predisposed ideas about people places or things. Unfortunately, they are also the most vulnerable to indoctrination. Small children trust their parents to explain the world to them, and they accept it unequivocally. Their beliefs and connection to a higher power are determined by that of their family, by the religion to which they belong, and by their perceptions of God and his teachings. In varying degrees, many religious sects fit the dynamics of a dysfunctional family, especially the most radical groups. In the psychology field of addictions specialty, we call the following dynamics religiosity, as it fits the addictive process of thinking. These dynamics in varying degrees are parallels of dysfunctional family parenting:

- They are a closed system with no room for discord or differences of opinion.
- They separate their members from the world at large and control what they are allowed to see, experience, and learn.
- They have rigid teachings of right and wrong and are perfectionists about what their members need to accomplish to gain God's approval.
- Their leaders, like some parents, often do not practice what they preach, which is a "crazy-making" behavior.

- They often use fear and shame, or manipulative communication, as weapons to control people, such as "You will go to Hell if you deviate from our teachings," or "You are always sinful."
- They threaten abandonment by telling people they are doomed without this.
- Some religions cut people off from their families and friends such as in the practice of shunning, along with the promise that they will not go to heaven if they deviate from this religion's particular interpretation of "God's word."
- There is an overwhelming lack of boundaries, insisting that these children who are now indoctrinated with fear follow their teaching.
- They play upon the human need to be special by telling people that they are the chosen, which creates feelings of superiority. This also teaches or implies that those who do not follow this path are doomed for eternity, or worse, that they are less valuable in the eyes of God. These religious sects, like dysfunctional families, are stuck in dysfunctional patterns, themes, and beliefs, which go back for generations and do not allow for fresh ideas, modern-day scientific facts, or any change in their belief system.

Members in many religions are referred to as the flock and the leaders as the shepherds. In these religious systems, the flock is not allowed to give input, just as children in dysfunctional homes have no voice. In many cases, there has been history of excessive use of verbal, physical, and sexual abuse, and preying upon the members who have less power, and believe that these religious leaders are infallible. In dysfunctional families, rigid and controlling parents also believe that they are infallible.

When there is sexual abuse, it is the most life-changing example of role reversal, where the child takes care of the adult's needs at their expense.

Belonging to and subscribing to many religions, especially the very radical ones, require the excessive use of denial, because historical research, facts, and even use of their entire biblical teachings do not match the belief system that they teach.

Rigid religious sects are extremely controlling of their members' thoughts, behaviors, and availability to learning and to new ideas. Essentially, they shut down the individual's ability to grow emotionally, intellectually, and spiritually.

In their rigid belief systems, they also often spawn deep prejudices and even hate toward those who are different. An example of this is found among fanatical religions. These are fear- and shame-based systems and can attract people who lack a fully developed self- actualization.

As a child, I was fortunate not to grow up in my father's family of origin, where they were fundamentalist Methodists. I do, however, have a few memories that involved their methods of teaching.

Once when I was very small, my father shamed me with criticism for saying "darn." Another example occurred when I spent a month with my father's older sister, who, like all of his family except himself, lived out in rural country. They were simple country folk, people descended from a long line of puritan ancestors who came to this country in poverty and worked other people's land. Several of my great uncles on my father's side became Methodist ministers. Some traveled around the countryside as visiting preachers in the poorer parishes. My grandfather, though not ordained, also was known to sometimes preach in his church.

During one particular summer, I lived with my aunt, who I have loved as the only grandmother figure I have known. I attended their little country church. After listening to a few "hellfire and brimstone" type sermons, I got saved. I was twelve years old, and

I thought that my father would be pleased upon returning home. Instead, I encountered both of my parents' disapproval.

As I hunted out revival meetings (we lived in town), and refused to watch television, or have anything to do with makeup or dancing, my parents had discussions about sending me to a psychiatrist! Naturally, this was a shock to me, not to mention very "crazy making". After all, this was my father's family, so why was he so disturbed? However, living in town, entering junior high school, and wanting to fit in did not go well with this religious path I had taken up. It lasted only about a year. During that year, I was isolated from other relationships, including my own family, because of the differences of beliefs.

Some people who are drawn to religion as adults, especially the type of religious group that offers to be "the chosen," find this appealing because they are not connected to Self, have grown up in dysfunctional families, and are looking for a place to feel they belong, to feel special.

At age twelve, I already fit very well into this category. I hated myself, as I felt that my mother hated me. Part of my susceptibility to this was the constant criticism and shaming that my mother had perpetrated through my early years. Though she really wasn't attached to any religion, this shaming fit right in with the evangelical church, which, in my experience, denigrates people and scares them more than they affirm. Affirming is only given if a follower conforms. I wanted to belong, to be among the chosen and also, unconsciously, wanted to get rid of the shame from my parents. I believed maybe I could get good enough by joining this religious path. There are many adults, much older than twelve, who seek these religions to find a place to belong, to feel chosen, and to rid themselves of shame — real or indoctrinated by the religion — even though they may not be aware of these motives. However, the greatest problem is that many of these religions function in such a way that their messages call for perfectionism. They are controlling in their doctrines, so that it is another perpetration on the Self. Perfectionism creates more shame. It is not possible to be perfect, and excusing mistakes by branding people as sinners only works to create more shame.

As I studied and grew, I looked at this in the larger view of each country and culture with their long-held and deeply ingrained beliefs and wondered: How do you justify only one belief system? Years later, when I asked my mother why they wanted to send me to a psychiatrist (because this was Daddy's family religion), she replied that she had lived with her in-laws during her early marriage and had not been affected this way. She compared my susceptibility as a child to hers as an adult. This has provided more evidence for me regarding how little my mother understood about children and how much more susceptible children are to indoctrination than are adults. Therefore, just as a child growing up in a Christian closed system will be brainwashed with those beliefs, so will a child in a Muslim closed system mentally incorporate those beliefs. A Jewish closed system will create the same outcome for their child, and so on. Remember I am talking about fanatic, radical fundamentalism, not every Christian, Jew, or Muslim.

Religious doctrine that speaks to creating healthy relationships is found in such teachings as "Love thy neighbour as thyself," which is written in some form in most all of the major religious teachings. *Thank goodness many religious systems are not closed, but instead are open, based on creating connection and unity among people with allowance for many spiritual paths.* Closed religious systems create disconnection of human beings from one another and ultimately lead to war. Do you know of any war that has not been justified by religious differences? Think of the Civil War, the American Revolution, Korea, and Vietnam.

Spirituality is an open system. It is related to the soul, the inner Self, rather than an external system. It is not bound by one or another interpretation but allows the individual to find and to express it in his/her personal way. It is a concept and experience of connecting to each other, rather than setting ourselves apart, as different, better, or as the chosen. The great value of churches, synagogues, temples, etc., is that they are gathering places for people to connect to their spiritual beliefs and TO EACH OTHER. Relationships can be formed that enhance their lives. These are very nurturing and often give hope to some who feel lost and hopeless.

Sarah, at age sixty-eight, had begun studying theological history and was stunned to find out that the story of Jesus was not necessarily THE TRUTH, as supported by facts. She learned, for example, that Christianity was founded some seventy years after Christ died. For many years, there were many versions of Christianity, mostly formed to fit in with the reigning political powers, such as Emperor Constantine. Politics and religion were enmeshed in those days, as they still are to a very great extent. At age sixty-eight, this was very disturbing for Sarah, as she had blindly followed her church's teachings for all those years and now felt she had no spiritual roots she could claim as her own. She was feeling depressed and scared that she wouldn't have enough time left to sort this out and find her spiritual path. It also meant looking at her relationship(s) with the church and many friends. There was fear of alienation if she deviated from these teachings.

Many religions call their priests or ministers by the name Father, which must be very confusing for a small child. In addition, God is referred to as The Father or Our Father. The child also has a father (Dad), so it is easy to attribute the same qualities that are experienced with Dad (father) to church priests, ministers, and God. Therefore, if Dad is mean, stern, unfair, frightening, angry, shaming, abusive, and unforgiving, as many are in dysfunctional families, then how can a child form a positive perception of God the Father? This also can intensify a child's perception of men in general and cause him/her to be closed to these relationships.

Also, some religious groups preach more about fear of an angry, vengeful God, than such as what Jesus and other ancient, revered, spiritual leaders actually taught and lived: love, kindness, forgiveness, and being one with others. Add to this, that there are religious leaders still practicing the use of anger, fear, and shaming to control their parishioners, rendering a child afraid to question or think outside the box.

Those religious groups who teach that war and killing are doing God's will, and that God is on their/our side are probably the greatest barrier to creating connected peaceful relationships that support each other. Without these peaceful relationships, connecting with others of different paths, we can be doomed to war after war after war. Certainly we know the gods were believed to take sides and to support war in ancient times. Have we not grown past this?

I am very fortunate, as I said before, that my exposure to religious separatism, as the perfect specimen of a needy adult child of two alcoholics, did not hold me there. I came to believe very simplistically that from the peaceful and loving teachings of the ancient teachers' teachings, such as "Love thy neighbor as thyself," that goodness is about how we live, behave, and treat ourselves and others. It is about healthy relationships. This makes such good sense to me. I also believe that the great prophets of all these major religions taught their version of the same concepts. Most have been distorted by man, not by their basic spiritual premises, often making relationship with religion another block to growth and connection with others, and with Self's own spiritual path. Today, we are at war with religious fanatics. It makes sense that we are inundated with FEAR in a global, fast-changing world. This is when the adult child can pull deeper into a closed system, whose beliefs promise more safety for those who follow their rigid manmade tenets about God. It can help control the fear. I am reminded of the movie "The Color Purple" when Celie says to Sophia in reference to men beating women, "We will all go to a better place soon." When we human beings feel out of control and scared, we look for black-and-white answers. In closed religious systems, you can find them. It is a way to hide. Then, they also blame the other religions of the world and advocate some version of eradicating them, such as the fundamentalist sect of Muslims with al-Qaeda; such as some of our radical fundamentalists, who advocate war to get rid of other fundamentalists, or such as blaming gay people for diseases or bad things that happen. Advocating war, hate, and eradication scares me more than any other threat. War begets tragedy and more war. Anger and fear of differences begets more of the same. History confirms this over and over. This is all about children from dysfunctional families, who have grown up wounded mentally, sexually, and physically, and who, instead of being able to love or tolerate others, fear them. Their relationship with religion sometimes can keep them from connecting and forming inclusive healthy relationships with other human beings.

In summary, your relationship with religion can sometimes greatly affect your choices in relationships with friends, community, family, children, schooling, global beliefs, and all areas of your life relationships.

QUESTIONNAIRE ON RELATIONSHIP WITH RELIGION

1. Did your family belong to a particular religious sect?
2. Was this an ancestral religion?
3. How many generations? Country of origin?
4. Were your parents of the same religion?
5. Did your parents practice their religion?
6. Do you practice this religion and/or identify with it?
7. Did your family practice religiosity? Radical fundamentalism?
8. What effect has religion or its absence had on your life?
9. Do you have friends/relationships that are from different religious backgrounds? Does this create conflict in the relationship?
10. Was/is your religion an open or closed system?

Chapter Nine

RELATIONSHIP WITH ANGER, ABANDONMENT, SHAME AND FEAR

Impounding Self-Esteem

It is pretty well-recognized in the field of psychotherapy, that adult children of dysfunctional families are largely fear-based. Here is where we can see the effects of our "family stew" in our lives, from our history of experiencing how anger, abandonment, shame, and fear were handled by our parents and other caretakers. This simply means that these families are unable to create a safe environment in which a child will be able to flourish, feel special and nurtured, and move toward self-actualization. Instead, the child becomes stuck in survival, which is an on-going theme in the family and is all about fear.

Fear is not all a bad thing, as there is some normal need of fear involved in survival. A healthy family will teach children things to fear or be careful of, such as in crossing streets, talking to strangers, being out after dark, certain people or situations, and other rational and reasonable things that we need to know to stay safe.

It is our personal relationship with fear that is so very important. In a dysfunctional home, there are many ways in which fear is created by such things as the parents' lack of healthy boundaries; outspoken prejudicial belief systems; parents' negative scary behaviors and harsh punishments including verbal, physical, and sexual abuse; adult friends who visit the home and are unsafe for the children; parental neglect; screaming and/or physical fights and threats between parents and siblings.

Children with a big out-of-control parent or bigger, older sibling will feel unprotected/unsafe. One of the most traumatic things is when parents do not believe the child and do not take action when the child reports that he/she has been abused by a parent, other sibling, neighbour, or at school. Many of you may recognize some or all of these conditions as having occurred in your early life, or you may have denied or repressed how really frightening your childhood was. Often children do that to preserve sanity when people and events are just too overwhelming. It can be part of repression, which I described in Chapter Fifteen: Denial. It can occur in a silent, secretive family, as well as in a chaotic, unpredictable one.

Be assured however, that you can get a true picture of your level of fear by examining your belief systems and behaviors as an adult, and how much you are driven by fear. Remember, today is full of symptoms from yesterday's traumas. Behaviors, such as avoiding opportunities that require change and the unknown, keeping busy all the time, talking a lot (which avoids feelings), addictions, very rigid routines, trying to control other people, along with other dysfunctional behaviors, reflects one being fear-based. We grow up with either a healthy or unhealthy relationship with fear.

Abandonment(s), shaming, and inappropriately expressed anger by caregivers creates an overload of fear. With too much fear, we are immobilized in much of our life, unable to take risks appropriately, and our creativity is stifled.

Finally, and very importantly, fear can prevent expression of joy, love, and other good feelings. Intimacy with another can be impossible because of deep-based fear.

Anger is really a secondary emotion, that occurs when we are hurt or frightened. Anger can allow us to feel more powerful at times, warning us of danger, or helping us protect ourselves in an abusive situation. We often feel anger first when we are scared, hurt, or in pain. We would hope to get angry rather than, frozen in fear, for example, if we or someone dear were being attacked or threatened. When our personal boundaries are violated by physical or verbal aggression, it is natural to feel anger first.

In dysfunctional families, there is often a lot of unpredictability, as for example, when there is an angry parent or other caregiver who rages, or an alcoholic or other person who is mentally unstable. We crave predictability to feel safe. Sometimes expression of anger is irresponsibly slimed all over everyone around, even though the anger is not directed at those who are witnessing it. Anger, combined with disciplinary actions, creates an overreaction to the behavior being disciplined, and usually the behavior is not distinguished from the Self of the child. Thus, "You did something bad" becomes "You are bad."

Physical and verbal abuse are laden with anger, which frightens and destroys the self-esteem of the child. Inappropriate, overreactive anger also can create a lot of "crazy making" for a child. One example is when a behavior is not reprimanded one day or had even been approved in the past, then another day the same behavior sets off rage in a parent. Another example is when the parent is angry, and the child doesn't know why or is too young to understand. For the child, this creates a need to develop private logic about why the parent is angry, so that he/she can somehow control or prevent this anger from reoccurring. Sadly, this private logic leads to a false conclusion, which often is that "It is my fault," rather than seeing the parent as wrong. It also can lead to forming an opinion that one of the parents is the good guy, and the other is the bad guy, a decision that later becomes a self-fulfilling prophesy in choosing mates and friends.

Inappropriately expressed anger is also very shaming, especially to a child. Shaming creates a tremendous amount of fear in a child and often leads to a shutdown in growth emotionally, and sometimes physically. Physical development shutdown is more prominent in women, especially where there is sexual abuse and/or incest. It creates shame and fear around their bodies, which makes them afraid of being a woman. (This is usually expressed with anorexia or obesity, to hide the body). Shaming happens when we are verbally, physically, or sexually abused, and if we are abandoned or neglected. The following issues in dysfunctional families create shame: poor boundaries, addictions, out-of-control anger, role reversals, looking good, closed systems, gender preferences, gossip, verbal, physical, and sexual abuse, abandonment, manipulative communication, perfectionism, and family enmeshment.

Children assume that whatever their caretakers do is appropriate, and that all caretakers do the same. The smaller the child, the more vulnerable he/she is to profound hurt, which can leave a wound for a lifetime. When abused, the vulnerable child will begin to shut down little by little and develop an Adaptive Self. The more powerless children feel, the more they need to adapt to dysfunction to avoid shame. As a result, there is more anger, fear, and shame internalized. If you have wondered why your anger seems at times to be inappropriate or overreactive going toward rage, it is because you are tapping into wounds of old internalized and unresolved anger and hurt from childhood. Adapting is the only way to survive when there is an overload of hurt, negativity, and lack of safety.

An example of a very shame-based family is Dawn's. She came from a very large family of ten children. The themes in the house were sexual violation and shame, along with a lot of parent/child role reversal, and a free-for-all and chaotic living style, because the mother was an alcoholic and the father a workaholic. The children operated as a unit in a chaotic way, developed a sibling abusive process, where older boys sexually abused their younger sisters, and they related with hitting, sarcasm, pranks, and generally unsafe behaviors. The parents were very unavailable; there was no safety.

At first, Dawn could not even identify with the concept of shame, having built a mental fantasy in childhood that denied the abuse, said it didn't affect her, and excused neglect on the part of the parents by understanding how difficult it was for them. Many of us do that — deny our hurts by feeling bad for parents. The telling factor for Dawn is how she repeated her childhood abuse in the relationships she set up in her adult life. She ended up sexually shamed, abandoned, used and alone, just like in her childhood.

Verbal and emotional abuse is highly underrated in their effect on children. Once I heard a workshop leader named Kay Smullens refer to emotional abuse as the invisible malignancy. I believe they are the worst abuses, because they create the deepest wounds in our self-esteem, creating negative concepts of Self. Rokelle Lerner, a well-known author regarding adult children, teaches that, "All it takes (for emotional wounding) is one critical parent."

Verbal abuse creates recordings of messages we repeat in our heads over and over throughout our lifetime, unless we work to erase them and re-record new ones that are positive and true. There are, according to statistics, twice as many suicides as there are homicides. I always have believed that suicide happens in a moment when the emotional pain is so overwhelming that one's logical mind freezes and is not able to see an alternative. Also, there seems to be no alternatives, because his/her head contains only negative beliefs about Self. This translates to hopelessness.

Dysfunctional families are loaded with verbal abuse, some of which is direct, such as name calling. Much of the abuse is messages that the child interprets from behaviors, facial expressions, body language of care-givers, and even from silence. Physical bruises and sexual perpetrators will go away, but the inherent shaming messages in these kinds of abuses will remain. Thus, all abuse involves verbal and emotional abuse, in messages the victim interprets from physical and/or sexual abuse.

In my childhood, although there were many other abusive elements, including sexual and all the fallout from this, I have come to the conclusion that what almost destroyed my self-esteem was the constant, verbal barrage of criticism my mother bombarded me with every day. To this day, I cannot remember even one incident in which she praised me for any achievement or for any simple act. Everything that I did and said seemed to meet with her disapproval. I am grateful for the fact that my personality has contained a tremendous amount of persistence to seek out therapy, to heal and to pursue my goals. I know that many children would not and do not emotionally survive that much verbal abuse.

Physical abuse teaches fear. It also teaches children to be physically abusive or to be vulnerable to this from bullies (physical abuse is a bullying behavior). "Spare the rod and spoil the child" is still believed by some parents. Unfortunately, it neither spares the child's self-esteem, nor gains respect for the caregiver but only teaches fear and internalized anger. As I said before, it also is shaming with an inherent message that gets locked into the child's self-esteem. Discipline with anger is always a way in which the caregiver is dipping into their unresolved anger wounds and perpetrating them into another generation.

Sexual abuse violates all of one's boundaries. It is the most devastating when it happens within the family, especially with one of the caregivers. It stifles and distorts normal sexual development of one's feelings about the body, about men and women, and especially about the value of Self. It permeates the entire being with shame. Sexual abuse not only creates a life of dysfunction around sex but also creates an overload of shame surrounding esteem of Self. Children almost always take on the shame of the perpetrator, particularly when the body (which is naturally designed to feel genital pleasure) can have a positive response to the feel of the abuse. This, combined with the discomfort and shamed feeling of being sexual with someone who is supposed to be a safe caretaker,

Anne Salter, LCSW

creates great distortions. As I have said earlier, the sexual abuse that I endured with my father has had profound effects in my adult life. These include my view of myself as a woman and my view of men. For many years, I believed that being sexy was what I needed to be wanted by anyone. I chose men who used me.

I often have heard a client describe abuses, including sexual violations, and then say, "I thought it was normal in families, even though it felt wrong." Little children think whatever the behavior is, whatever the ideas and practices are in their family are the norm. How could they think otherwise? Among other things, being sexually perpetrated creates a great amount of fear. (I will discuss this more in Chapter Twelve: Sexual and Emotional Intimacy.

Finally, issues of abandonment greatly damage self-esteem and create inordinate amounts of fear. This fear gets generalized by the child to the world, making it appear to be very unsafe. It also often creates panic attacks later in life, a tendency to cling to relationships or to avoid them, and to over-protect or under-protect one's own children.

One's ability to trust, after these betrayals by those most trusted, will be shut down and globalized to all people, especially those of the same gender as the perpetrators. In many cases, where a father has abused his child and the mother turned a blind eye or did not believe the child, then the globalization of mistrust will be directed at everyone, both male and female.

Certainly, abandonment can be physical, but most of us have not been left on a doorstep. Some of you, though, may have been adopted, sent to live with relatives or neighbors for a period of time, sent to boarding school under the age of fourteen or fifteen, punished by being locked out of the house, spent time in an orphanage, been locked in a closet, attic, or have been latch-key children, to name some physical abandonments. These forms of abandonment also can have a profound impact, creating fear of loss, loss of trust, withdrawal from people, and unresolved attachment.

Henry was traumatized at age ten, when his mother and father divorced and she moved out of the house. He already had experienced an overload of unpredictable levels of safety, being the youngest of four, very competitive siblings, who were vying for what little attention and nurture were available from two alcoholic and argumentative parents. He begged his mother not to leave. Soon, he began to eat as a way to medicate his fear and pain of loss. As a grownup, he suffers with post-traumatic stress syndrome, symptoms of depression, over-controlling behaviors, difficulty sleeping, an overeating disorder, and irrational fears of death. At times his fears and constant vigilance make him irritable and even full of rage. As a result, he always apologizes to his family for losing patience and then feels more shame. He has a lot of control issues, which negatively affect his relationships and have caused him, at times, to quit and/or be let go from work. These are the symptoms that are the fallout from childhood abandonment and sibling abuse at a young age, and the resulting overload of fear. These types of traumas often stunt the emotional growth of the child at the age when the trauma occurs.

Emotional abandonment can be just as wounding or even possibly more so than physical abandonment. Both create enormous fear in the child regarding his/her well-being, and cut deeply into self-worth. Parents can show their anger and disapproval by cutting off the child emotionally, as described in Chapter Three: Themes from our Family of Origin. This is done by not acknowledging the child's presence, not speaking to the child, or simply being cold and distant. For very small children, this is particularly devastating, as loss of a parent in this way feels like death. Some parents relate frequently in this way. It also can be "crazy making," as sometimes the child does not know why it is happening, and the parent will not tell them. This was a constant in my life since I was very young.

Abandonments, along with irresponsible expression of anger and shaming, create inordinate amounts of fear in a child. The child then becomes stifled in the business of growing up emotionally, and being able to evolve into a unique, individual

Self. If these wounds are not healed, then it is impossible to form healthy relationships as an adult.

QUESTIONNAIRE ON RELATIONSHIP WITH ANGER, ABANDONMENT, SHAME, AND FEAR

1. How was anger expressed in your family? By Dad? By Mom? By others?
2. Did you grow up in an angry household? Was anyone a rager?
3. Were children allowed to express anger?
4. Share ways in which you experienced abandonment emotionally, physically, and spiritually.
5. Were you a latch-key child? Did the adults work outside of the home?
6. What kinds of shaming did you experience as a child? How does that affect you today?
7. Describe what you know about your own fearfulness. Does it prevent you from risk taking, such as travel? Changing jobs? Getting more schooling? Does it cause you to isolate?
8. Who were you afraid of in your childhood?
9. Are you often irritable? Angry? Do people say you are? Do you believe you are fear-based?

Chapter Ten

RELATIONSHIP WITH TEACHERS AND SCHOOL-MATES

Another Chance or More Wounding?

When a child starts school, it is an opportunity to hugely expand his/her world. Or, it may shut him/her down to the world if it doesn't feel safe. By now, you are aware that we carry our emotional baggage with us. This includes many stored wounds, traumas, and already formed ideas about whether people and the world are safe. We have consumed most of our parent's beliefs and prejudices about people, places, and things. And, most of all, we have learned to trust or not trust men and women by how we

experienced our parents, religious leaders, and/or other caretakers. The teacher is the second opportunity we have for the formation of a valued Self, belief in the Self, and in learning to flourish in relationships. It is a chance to learn some discernment of people, places, and things, and that everything is not black and white, good or bad, or safe or unsafe. This lack of discernment represents a common dysfunction in adult children. A kind teacher can be an angel in a child's life.

Although we are the intelligent species, it has taken us centuries to recognize in school and in many other areas of life that children aren't stamped out of cookie cutters. We are unique individuals in a myriad of ways and cannot get the same outcome by treating everyone as if they are all the same. This has been especially tragic in the school system, where for centuries there has been a tendency to educate children at the same rate, without regard to individual needs and abilities. This lack of individualizing children during the education process creates some or all of the following: boredom, shame, and giving up. It also has been a tragedy that certain human beings have been branded with stereotypes, which create prejudice. This prejudice is so hard to overcome, because we store our early beliefs so deeply in our being.

The teacher often is faced with not only the task of preparing and teaching specific subjects, but also of trying to reach and interest young children in learning. Children, who come from unpredictable homes where they do not feel safe, will usually either act out or withdraw and shut down by staring out a window while lost in fantasy. They are emotionally on fear overload and sometimes worried about what is happening at home, after, for example, last night's crisis of some kind, for which they got no reassurance. They have no energy or available attention for school. If they then experience negative input at school, such as rigid chastisement for not paying attention, it only will deepen the problems that they are having and lessen any chance of learning. If, on the other hand, some kind and patient teacher, who is emotionally mature, takes a special interest, he or she can end up being that angel in the child's life, reawakening the child's natural curiosity, and helping to motivate him/her into functioning well and going on to achieve success.

Louise had a life-changing experience in the third grade. Up until then, she had experienced mostly positive relationships at school. Then, at age eight, she had a teacher who seemed, in retrospect, to have been mentally off-balance. She took food out of the children's lunch boxes and did other weird things. Worst of all, she terrorized and shamed Louise. She made fun of her curly hair, so that Louise grew up hating her hair despite compliments and even envy from others. This teacher once refused to let her go to the bathroom. Louise then urinated on herself and was humiliated horribly. Though Louise was not one to complain, she tried to tell her mother about how crazy and hurtful this teacher was, but her mother thought this church school could do no wrong. The fact that her mother did not believe her or take action added to the trauma. From these experiences, Louise grew up with scars to her self-esteem, which turned out to be some of the most painful wounds she worked through in therapy.

I have a friend who grew up in a very abusive family and whose life was changed by a teacher who took a special interest in her, recognized her special abilities in mathematics, encouraged and vouched for her, and helped to get her a college scholarship. She was able to go on and to become a very successful accountant, as a result of this teacher's interest and encouragement. It was that one special person who showed her that she mattered and helped her begin to believe in herself.

School experiences always play a major part in forming our relationships with our Self and others. These experiences also add to our repertoire of relationship experiences with authority figures. Many children, who had negative relationships with adult authority figures, have difficulty with authority figures when they become adults. We learn about relationships at school in so many ways. Sometimes, they just reinforce the negatives that we have experienced at home. Sometimes, as I did myself, we can form positive relationships at school, even though the ones at home are negative. In this case, we may love school and see it as a sanctuary. Though it will not replace the approval we innately need from our parents, many times it can boost our self-esteem and open up possibilities, which seem impossible at home. An affirming teacher can encourage us to succeed, even if it only plants a seed.

Forming good relationships with our classmates can give us invaluable groundwork for future friends and job relationships. However, children can be very mean to each other. I believe most of this is about power. We are powerless at home as children, and if we are abused by our parents or our siblings, we internalize anger and develop a need to have power, or alternately, a victim role.

From the "Family Stew" sometimes emerges a child, who has been bullied by a parent, taking on the role of a bully. The school bully is a child who has been abused at home. This child has been excessively yelled at, punished, and put down in general. He/she then goes to school and picks on those smaller or less powerful children to feel powerful. In so doing, the child vents the internal hurt and rage, which really belongs at home. It is particularly sad when children learn at home that the meaning of power is to be abusive to others. In fact, the bully is exhibiting being powerless over his own anger. Children who form gangs have been abused and deprived. While acting fearless gives bullies a feeling of power, in fact, they are actually full of fear themselves.

Being bullied at school is another way in which a less aggressive child will lose more self-esteem, dislike school, feel unprotected like he does at home, and perhaps give up on academics. The bully also will collect more internal pain from hurting others, from often being in trouble, and from being shamed and punished at school. Safety is such an important factor for us, even more so for little children. If we do not feel safe, we end up using our energy to adapt and to survive, which results in our inability to function.

If we have an affirming teacher, then school can feel safer than home, because there are boundaries and perhaps no "crazy making" or verbal abuse. It also can be that one lives in a chaotic, unpredictable home, and school offers predictability and clear boundaries. In this case, it lets us know that there are boundaries and safe places in the world — a lesson in discernment. This then gives us one of the greatest chances to grow up not viewing the world as if it's the same as our dysfunctional family of origin. It may open up a child from a shutdown position, so they can gain some trust and, therefore, take a risk in order to connect in relationship. Without this positive experience with a teacher, the child may remain shut-down and afraid of relationships. With proper encouragement, a child can begin to want to explore new ideas and his/her talents despite the abuse, closed system of ideas, or disinterest that may exist in the home. School is an open system in which to explore new horizons. Thus, teachers and positive school experiences have the best shot at becoming a positive ingredient in the stew, which forms us as individuals.

QUESTIONNAIRE ON SCHOOL HISTORY

1. Describe how your family viewed and dealt with education. Were they helpful and supportive?
2. Was education emphasized as important? If so, was it emphasized as equally important for boys and girls?
3. To what level were your parents educated? What kind of message(s) did you receive about your intelligence and abilities at home? Did your family's beliefs conflict with school?
4. Did you like school? Were you successful academically? Were you with other children/classmates? Did you attend school regularly? Discuss this.
5. Did you experiment with drugs and alcohol? When did you begin using mood-altering substances? Did you smoke cigarettes? When did you begin?
6. What do you remember most about school? What did you like best? Least?
7. Were you confident in going to school, or frightened? Describe your feelings.
8. Did you have special teachers? What did you gain from him/her?
9. Did you have any teacher(s) who you did not like or who were abusive? Discuss this.
10. How far did you go in school academically? Do you wish you had gone further?
11. Have you had other teachers/mentors in your life who influenced your feelings about yourself?
12. What do you believe about yourself in terms of intelligence and potential?
13. What kind of messages do you give yourself? Are they supportive?
14. Were you a bully? Or, were you bullied?

CHAPTER ELEVEN

RELATIONSHIP WITH FRIENDS

Effects of Lost Trust

E ssentially, there is always a lack of trust that increases over time in dysfunctional families. Parents or other caregivers reflect some or all of the following traits and behaviors: unpredictability, reneging on promises, sometimes even lying that promises were made, not being there for children's needs, abusive and scary at times, bringing unsafe people into the home, violating boundaries (worst of all, sexual), and giving a lot of double messages on the same subject.

First there is family, whether dysfunctional or not, with whom we have the deepest and most lasting internal relationships. Our next closest relationship will be in couple-ship, but before that are the friends we make. Some of us grow up having many friends and acquaintances, some dating back to childhood. Others have few or no friendships, often resulting from living in isolated areas as a child, or moving a lot, such as a military family. In addition, we have different personality predispositions and adaptations to early relationships (roles). For example, someone in a lost child role is less likely to have a load of friendships. A more outgoing child in the hero role may overcome these issues more easily. Growing up in a dysfunctional family with birth parents doesn't eliminate the danger of losing trust in early life. The main ingredient needed for any infant/child is a feeling of safety and predictability. This is a time that really speaks to the importance of behaviors over words. The caretaker's behaviors are all a child can relate to. I realize I am repeating some of what I said in Chapter One, but it is purposeful to emphasize the importance of trust in forming close relationships.

As children grow and begin to understand words, in addition to behaviors, the trust issue becomes more complex. Now, if behaviors and words are not congruent, such as if I tell a child that I am not angry, but I have an angry affect and behave in threatening ways, then I will create confusion and lack of trust. Thus, in dysfunctional chaotic families, there are a lot of incongruent words and behaviors.

It is important to add that siblings also certainly can contribute to the destruction of trust, where they have done such things as tricking each other, sexually violating each other, tattling on each other and/or physically hurting each other, etc.

The end result is that growing up in these families means carrying a good amount of fear of trusting people. Now let's look at how these early relationships affect our choosing, or not choosing of friends. No doubt, you already can see how making close friendships will be difficult with more pitfalls when trust has been so violated by people who were supposed to be the safest: family. A good, healthy friendship should include a lot of trust, feeling safe to be with someone, being able to share our intimate feelings about life, about our needs, our hopes, and dreams. It should be comfortable and safe to work through differences and arguments.

Sometimes, one may continue a friendship from early childhood, but as both people have gone their separate paths (beliefs, philosophies, spiritual choices), the ability to share and explore everything is not prudent in this relationship. However, there can be large pieces of safe and available avenues to still enjoy in this friendship. Hopefully, both people now have newer friends with whom other values and interests are more congruent. Many times friendships are not really that, but are merely acquaintances we pick up and then discard. People often will say, "Billy is a good friend of mine," when in fact, Billy is simply a fellow employee or a relationship of temporary convenience, but not one where there is real commitment. These acquaintances are sometimes described as friends, because there is no real understanding of what a true friend would be like. There is no understanding or learned skills from the family of origin to know how to form a true friendship. Such a relationship consists of trust, honesty, an unwritten commitment to be there for each other whenever possible, an on-going enjoyment of each other's company, and a heart connection with each other (without any sexual involvement). It is the way one would experience a healthy family and one step short of a committed relationship in couple-ship. However, a true friendship does not have to involve years of living near each other (as would a couple-ship), but can be held onto over distances, and sometimes more infrequent face-to-face meetings.

Loneliness is a problem most adult children suffer. It is a longing for connection. When there has been no deep and safe connection in family of origin, it is impossible to know how to create one outside of the home. There is also fear that any connection might result in the kind of hurt and violations that were experienced in the family. There is a lack of trust. Therefore, what is the most needed — the nurture of a safe and fulfilling relationship of friendship — becomes another loss. Lost children experience this loneliness the worst. They were "the watcher" in the family, avoiding as much contact and involvement as possible, and forming very cynical impressions and beliefs about people, having globalized their home experience. Therefore, these children seldom will even attempt to form friendships and remain isolated; even in a couple-ship.

The hero child will seem to have many friends, but in fact, has no secure belief that these friends would be there if the hero were not always the giver. This hero role also holds a lot of resentment about their needs not being met, as they are only able to do for others and not able to receive. And, they usually choose people who are more takers. The scapegoat child, like the lost child, will be cynical about people and mostly is a taker, believing that he/she is entitled, because he/she was the recipient of so much family abuse. The scapegoat is more likely to use people to their benefit, a one-way relationship because of the extreme neediness this role creates, not knowing that this is not true friendship. Finally, the mascot child often uses so much humor and is so frenetic, that it is difficult to get close to him/her or have a serious connection.

These role behaviors result from fear, lost trust, and lack of positive, healthy, relationship skills. Whatever types of friendships they form, they will match up with other adult children, who also lack skills. In this way, they may repeat many of the abuses that were experienced in family of origin, such as abandonment, anger used as control in the relationship, and any and all of the co-dependent behaviors.

Sadly, we usually don't form really healthy and functional friendships as adult children, until we do recovery work. Again, this is due to the tendency to choose people, especially those we want to be close to, out of transference from our family of origin. When we find ourselves in painful relationship glitches in a friendship, we usually can (if we look) see that we are seeming to replicate behaviors of mom, dad, or a sibling with whom we have unfinished business

Sometimes, though, we bond with our similar emotional wounds or with someone with whom we connect in fun or other interests, such as in childhood and teenage years. This, also coming out of our "stew," can help us emotionally survive. I consider these friends to be angels in our lives.

QUESTIONNAIRE ON RELATIONSHIP WITH FRIENDS

1. Do you feel you have friends you can trust? How many?
2. Do you have one or more friends who would be there for you in a real crisis?
3. Have you been betrayed by a close friend? Is it a pattern?
4. Do you have a best friend? How often do you have contact?
5. As an adult, are most or all of your friends living in another location far away? Are your real friends only from where you were raised?
6. Do you have trouble making friends? If so, do you know why?
7. Can you relate your functioning in friendships to your family-of-origin experiences?
8. Do you find sometimes that a close friend relates to you as a family-of-origin member did? (Example, your mother was critical; your friend is critical.)

Chapter Twelve

RELATIONSHIP WITH SEXUALITY AND EMOTIONAL INTIMACY

Creates our Sexual Functionality

O ur sexual development and identity are such critical aspects of our lives, so it is important to understand how we can and do get off the natural track of development, and end up with negativity and fear about our sexual Self. Then, we end up missing out on the wonderful gifts of pleasure (without shame) that we are meant to have. Most of this has to do with inappropriate relationships in our family of origin, or some other inappropriate sexual experience in which we originally were sexually energized.

I have no doubt that the concept of sex and sexuality is the most misunderstood, distorted, and often hurtful or unrewarding reality in our human lives. These distortions cause it to often be a negative and confusing issue and are tied directly to our self-esteem. They come from what we learn about it, how our society deals with and abuses it, and our experiences around it while growing up. Sex is laughed at, flaunted, sold, abused, and connected to other issues of our self-esteem, such as how perfect and, therefore, appealing we believe that our bodies are. However, sex is really one of our greatest gifts. I believe that it is meant to be enjoyed as an expression of love as a healthy release and a joyful way of connecting to another human being. It is also how we keep creating life!

So, why do we have such a negative and confusing relationship with our sexuality? Everyone has sexuality. It is core to our being. We are born either a male or female physically. Most people are predisposed to an orientation of either heterosexual, attracted to opposite sex, or homosexual, attracted to same sex. Some do not feel the same gender orientation that their genitals designate. All of these can be one or both a result of nature and nurture input. For many, sexual orientation continues to be a very conflicted and fear-based issue, causing much unhappiness and unhealthy outcomes. However, creation happened, we are each gifted with a phenomenally intricate body, which, if not terribly abused, can give us great pleasure. Unfortunately, for some unfathomable reason, human beings (the most intelligent species) have managed to abuse this gift by distorting it. This has come out of sexual dysfunction and has been handed down over centuries. We have tried to control sex, as was done in the Victorian age by strict rules of conduct, how one is expected to dress, very often by religious groups claiming it as sinful and unclean, and during the Spanish Inquisition by torture.

Most of the negativity and "crazy making" has been directed at women. "BE SEXY!!!" — or — "NO, DON'T DARE BE SEXY!!!" Back and forth, we have gone from dress styles that hide all but the feet and the head, to styles that are almost totally nude. And, in more extreme styles, many women's faces are hidden in the Middle East. We are afraid of our sexuality, because it has been drummed into us for years, mainly by religion, that it is sinful or dangerous.

In my generation, girls were expected to control their sexual drive and the sexual drive of boys, and to remain chaste until married. It was believed that boys/men have no control over their libido, so boys would be expected to be looser sexually than girls/

women. It also was believed that a girl was a slut if she went too far, and that she would never find a husband if she had sex. Today, we have gone to opposite extremes, where we find thirteen- and fourteen-year-old girls being expected to have sex whenever they choose or are coerced. The idea of a thirteen-year-old girl choosing something she is so little informed about and unprepared for is a bit of an oxymoron! We do swing from one extreme to the other!

The ways in which we have attempted to control sex only have sent it underground, creating the very unnatural, excessive, and abusive practices that we so fear. Deprivation and shaming create excess, distortions, and abuse. There is widespread sex addiction, much of it fueled and enabled by pornography and the Internet.

Much of our society behaves as if they expect we would have orgies all the time if not controlled or supervised. Why don't we understand that these attempts to control are shaming? I believe that this same type of thinking permeates our fear of homosexuality; if you don't control it/them, then everyone will want to be homosexual. What?? Why?? Why would anyone choose to be part of something that sets them apart as different in ways that deny those rights that other citizens have and makes it harder to feel they belong and to live a fulfilling life?

In my practice, I rarely encounter anyone who seems to have a healthy sex life. Some have been scared away from it by admonishments and scare tactics, such as; "You will get pregnant," or "All that boys want from you is sex!" Others have been indoctrinated by a religion that preaches that sex is bad, sinful, or only for procreation. Still others have experienced, heard, or witnessed some form of sexual abuse or situation that was inappropriate for them at a young age or with a family member. Many people have experienced a combination of these things. Thus, sexuality and natural sexual flow becomes confused, distorted, and even frightening. Naturally, trust issues greatly play into the sexual act, as it involves a totally letting go in the experience of orgasm. If there are trust issues, this can greatly interfere with sexual release and pleasure, and, more importantly, with emotional intimacy.

Our sexuality and curiosity about it develops at a very young age. It is natural for a child to explore his/her body and to recognize some of the areas that produce pleasure. It also is natural to be curious about our body, other bodies, and especially those of other similar-age children. It is unlikely, however, that a child will become preoccupied with sex or sex-related pursuits before puberty, unless unhealthy circumstances happen, such as inappropriate touching, being abused, witnessing adult sexual activities, and other out-of-boundary activities or conversations which either frighten or cause the child to shift focus from normal childhood interests. Certainly, one who discovers that he/she is attracted to the same sex and hears the negative societal messages about the gay and lesbian lifestyle usually is going to be especially preoccupied with secrecy, fear, and shame.

I believe affairs and certainly sex addictions are an outcome of early life boundary violations in relationship, another outcome from our "family stew." If our first experience with sex is inappropriately energized with boundary violations, such as incest and other previously mentioned violations, then we will be attracted to crossing relationship boundaries, such as marriages and other committed relationships. We will lose our boundaries in general, because sexuality is so core to Self. Certainly, this can sometimes alter our sexual attractions to have confusing mixes of gay and straight attractions.

Unfortunately, part of the sexual revolution encourages not having many boundaries. No doubt this has added impetus to increased divorce and the tendency to not want to work on relationships. Intimate, committed relationships require work, like tending a garden. Sometimes, the still prevalent aura of shame that surrounds sexuality makes it difficult to talk about and to explore within the couple-ship, or even with a professional. When you have been violated, your sexual Self becomes a reservoir of shame. This impacts the ability to be emotionally intimate, which turns sex into a detached physical act, lacking heart connection to the partner. If couples do not have awareness of the development of their sexual selves and in what ways they were energized, they will have trouble working through emotional blocks. The most frequent examples of this are when one (or both) have been sexually abused or is a victim of incest. Even if there is conscious awareness of their history, there is almost always a ton of shame surrounding it, even though they were the victim. This is certainly one of those areas where there is need of professional help to move toward recovery.

Besides being sexually molested by my father at a very early age, which I repressed, there were other dysfunctional things that happened in my home regarding sex. I had a babysitter, who told me that old men have sex with little girls and hang them up bloody on trees. I was eight years old, so imagine how much fear this added to my experiences with my father, who was an old man to an eight-year-old. Also around the same age, my mother took me to see a movie called, Johnnie Belinda, a pretty explicit (especially for the 1940s) movie for those days, in which an older man raped a deaf, mute girl and then she had a baby. As an adult, I had a lot of fear and very dysfunctional sexual relationships wherein I usually needed to be medicated with alcohol or chose men who were unavailable for an intimate and lasting relationship. I was attracted to married men, because this mirrored my relationship with my father, in terms of the boundary violations. There are many symptoms of having been sexually abused, which show up in our adulthood. This can include trouble going to bed at night, having to be heavily covered up when in bed (regardless of temperature), getting up in the night to check the locks many times, needing the room very dark or a light on, difficulty having sex without some form of mood-altering drug, dressing in sexually explicit ways, difficulty having orgasm, flashbacks that occur during sexual activity, and many more.

The most devastating thing that sexual abuse or incest creates is a separation of heart and genitals. This is how a child reconciles Self to the boundary violation of a parent or other trusted caretaker/mentor, with whom he/she is originally emotionally intimate, and who has now become a sexual perpetrator. The child also will take on the shame, to maintain love or tolerance for the caretaker. Often, the child will repress the sexual abuse, to not be aware of something that is so very confusing, hurtful, and shameful. The sexual abuse or incest then creates a split of heart and genitals, causing the child to grow up incapable of connecting heart/emotional intimacy with sexual relationships.

I have heard many other versions of how people have gotten inappropriately sexually energized and how it has led to years of sexual disappointment, and in many cases distaste for one's own body. Here are some stories:

Patricia was not aware of sexual abuse or incest growing up. However, she was profoundly affected by some less direct sexual incidents in her childhood. As a young girl, she was uncomfortable with her mother wearing very skimpy lingerie around the house. She wanted to tell her mom to cover up more. Often for a child, it is overwhelming to see too much of an adult sexually exposed, especially during puberty. Then, at age twelve while looking for hidden Christmas presents, Patricia came across a whole pile of pictures of her parents in all sorts of nude and suggestive positions. She was horrified. She never told anyone until she was in therapy. Her symptoms have been extreme uncomfortability with her body (does not like to even look at it and is very critical of it) and those same symptoms I described in my story of being attracted to the unavailable, but not attracted to married or committed sex. The pictures actually traumatized her, seeing her parents in such a graphic sexual way, and she associates the trauma with married sex. Naturally, she married a man who preferred to walk around the house nude, which constantly freaked her out and reinforced her trauma. Being inappropriately sexually energized is a huge factor that creates much dysfunction in couple-ship and marriage and also leads some people into sex addiction or sexual anorexia.

Veronica, whose alcoholic father raped her at age five, also was fondled by a priest when she was a young teenager. He was a well-respected friend of the family. She grew up choosing men who abandoned her, and she married an alcoholic, who was also a sex addict and unfaithful. When she lost her second child and was in a terrible depression, the same priest who had fondled her as a child had sex with her under the guise of comforting her. She has carried a load of sexual shame, as do most victims of incest and sexual abuse, and has had trouble functioning sexually because of the trauma wounds around her sexual Self. With support in her therapy, she finally wrote a letter to the church monsignor about this abusive priest. This was very hard for her, as she had held the shame for this abuse. It was hard for her to understand that even when one is an adult, especially if he/she was sexually abused as a child, that the difference in power position makes one vulnerable.

This is finally becoming recognized, as in my professional organizations who forbid personal business and especially sexual relationships between therapist and client/patient. It also is being recognized in schools, even when the student is in college. Anytime there is imbalance of power, it is inappropriate and cannot be deemed as two consenting adults.

Peter grew up in a home where no child was safe. His mother was an angry male-hating woman, who was left with three children when Peter's young father died of tuberculosis, or so he was told. Peter later learned that his father actually committed suicide. Peter grew up with his mother, one aunt, a matriarchal controlling grandmother, and five uncles, who had no wives. They were all sexual perpetrators. Peter was a victim of incest as a young boy. He was lured in with candy and a promise of much-needed attention. By puberty, Peter realized that he was gay and already felt a lot of shame and secretiveness about this. It further identified him with his uncles, because they were having homosexual sex with him.

When he was in junior high, some kids teased him about looking gay. From then on, he practiced looking straight in how he dressed, walked, and talked. He lived in constant fear of being discovered. As a result, he became asexual, or what today we call, sexually anorexic. He completely rejected himself as a sexual being. He chose a specialty area in his profession that mostly isolated him.

He dressed very conservatively and still is very careful not to show possible signs of being gay. Eventually, by exploring and healing much of this in therapy, he was able to have a gay committed relationship, but he still struggles with secretiveness about this very intimate part of himself.

Maggie grew up in a very non-communicative home with an unhappy mother, who smoked heavily. There was no sexual abuse that she knows of, but in many ways what happened to her was worse. It came out of neglect and not being protected by parents who were not really connected to their children. When Maggie was nine years old, her parents' best friend's sixteen-year-old son began to have intercourse with her. She was very vulnerable because she needed attention, along with being so young. Also, to add to this betrayal, his sister was her best friend and probably was sacrificing Maggie to her brother to protect herself. Attention at home was non-existent. And, because the family did not communicate, especially about anything negative, she did not tell them. Also, because his family was her parents' best friends, she worried about how they would feel. At nine years old, we are really limited in our understanding and often assume if something happens to us, that it must be the way things work or the way of the world. Add to this that children take on the blame and shame when they are sexually perpetrated.

This boy continued to have sex with her for five years, until she was fourteen. There had to have been symptoms, but her family never noticed. She took on all of the shame. She became over-energized sexually. As a young teenager, she began to be more sexually provocative than her friends, even when they seemed dismayed. She didn't understand why. This added more shame to her inner Self. She lived in a mental bubble. At age seventeen, Maggie became pregnant by another boy, and, in her family's fashion, she continued to function externally as if nothing were different, including attending school pregnant. She was extremely traumatized with shame and wondered why she was so bad.

There was a lot of silent shaming in her family. The baby was given up for adoption and never mentioned again. She developed a powerful inner critic, which kept ripping at her self-esteem. She was also in a family who belonged to a rather rigid sexually shaming religion. As an adult, she developed several addictions, including sex. She married, but had numerous affairs and abortions. This continued to blacken her self-image, adding to her wounded child. She has made good recovery with her other addictions but still struggles with the sexual compulsion, because it comes from such a deep childhood wound. Much of the wound was created by parental neglect. For many years, she was afraid to tell her parents about the boy who inappropriately sexualized her at a young age and how this set her on a sexually destructive life path. This all but destroyed her self-esteem and gave her many years of emotional pain, and an unfulfilling marriage.

Janie has so much sexual anxiety that she cannot even date. She sometimes makes a date just to have sex and has to get very inebriated. Of course, she never gets pleasure or release from it, only more shame. Her sexual shame began when she was only four, when her grandfather made her fondle him. Then, growing up in a boundary-free home with out-of-control addicted parents and four siblings, she was emotionally sexually abused by learning about her dad's affairs and by hearing her parents have sex when she was in the same room with them on a road trip. Her history has included no committed relationships and no rewarding sexual experiences. Her relationship with her sexual Self is negative and loaded with fear.

Paul grew up in a family of six children, with a mother who seemed to hate men and sex, and a father who was unavailable whether at work or at home. He had three sisters who taunted and teased him, calling him names and leaving him out of their activities. His mother told him that girls were special and he had to treat them nice. This was very conflicting, because his sisters were so mean to him. Paul had no one to guide him sexually (with a very passive father), and he lived in a house full of girls, along with a young housekeeper. At ages twelve and thirteen, when his sexual curiosity began to peak, he would peep through the keyhole at the young housekeeper. His mother caught him and told him he was evil, and asked him how he could do this, because the housekeeper was such an angel. His sisters began to lock their doors, as if he were some sort of pervert. Paul was a talented artist, so he began drawing naked girls to deal with his curiosity. He hid the pictures and some sexy magazines under his rug. His behaviors were normal for a young man. Through trickery by his sisters, he got set up and blindsided by his mother, who found the hidden magazines and the naked drawings. She beat him with a belt and told him he was despicable and sick. (He also had heard her say the same thing about him to his father). Not only was Paul's self-esteem destroyed by being the scapegoat of his mother and sisters, but his sexual development was fraught with trauma. His mother decided that the way to give him sex education was to take him out to witness two dogs mating, an experience that he felt humiliated and shamed by.

As a result, Paul was unable to form a sexually intimate relationship. When his wife rejected his sexual overtures, he started having affairs and quickly developed a sex addiction. His sexuality was infused with anger, and he used it to feel powerful, by manipulating women with the pleasure he trained himself to give. The addiction and self-hatred was so strong that it took being arrested to get him into recovery. He is now a middle-aged man who is afraid to date. He never had a father or male mentor to help him develop sexually in a positive and normal way, nor was his self-esteem good enough to date and to develop a positive sense of himself as a man.

These are examples of how our sexual Self is formed at a very early age. If our sexuality gets energized through sexual trauma, then we will have problems being sexually functional in rewarding ways. Our relationship with our sexuality will be distorted and negative. Many times, much of our early sexual experience is buried in our unconscious. There is so much shame around it that we need professional help to become healthy. This is such a very important part of Self. Our relationship with our sexual Self is a core part of how we are able to function in any potentially intimate relationship and a core part of our self-esteem. If we are wounded as a child in the area of our sexuality, then our sexual self-esteem and development will be arrested and distorted, stored away in our locker of wounds, yet fully influencing our relationships.

Questionnaire on Relationship with Sexuality

1. Do you know how you were originally sexually energized? Explain.
2. Are you aware of sexual abuse or incest that you suffered?
3. Are you aware of sexual abuse in your family? Parents and/or siblings?
4. Were there indications in your family of inappropriate sexual energy or behavior?
5. Was there emotional incest or discomfort in your home?
6. Did you have a role of little wife, or little husband?
7. Were your parents openly affectionate?
8. Were you aware of your parents' sexual relationship?
9. Did you experience any form of sexual abuse, rape, or inappropriate sexual overtones growing up?
10. Did you know your grandparents and other relatives, and was there history of sexual abuse or inappropriate touching or other behaviors?
11. What was your experience about your sexual Self at school?
12. Do you minimize any uncomfortable sexual experience in your life?
13. How are/have been your sexual experiences as an adult?
14. Do you struggle with sexual relations as an adult? In what ways?
15. Do you identify yourself as heterosexual, homosexual, bisexual, or other?
16. Do you have any siblings or close relatives who do not identify as heterosexual? Was this a problem in your family?

Chapter Thirteen

RELATIONSHIP WITH SELF

Wounded and Adapted/Childhood Decisions

W e have reviewed the major influences from our "family stew" in our personal development. We also have looked at other major influences, such as teachers, relatives, religious leaders and their indoctrinations, and negative experiences that create trauma wounds. These influences mostly occur in our first six to ten years of age and form our most deeply held beliefs and attitudes, whether we are in agreement or disagreement with these influential sources. From these influences, we form our prejudices and some of our childhood decisions that sabotage us later in life. This book explores, in some depth, how our relationship with people, places, and things reflects our lack of a healthy relationship with Self. This, in turn, affects our relationships and is symptomatic of childhood wounds. My goal throughout this book is to show how other relationships that we form, as we go through life, can continue to wound Self. Now, we will look at how our relationship with Self has been formed from our relationships with these people and experiences.

One's relationship with Self will form the heart of one's ability to have meaningful, functional, fulfilling relationships with the rest of the world. The parents' job is to help their child form a positive self-identity and to learn skills that will enable him/her to go forward in life pursuing his/her goals and dreams, which are suited to an inherent unique Self. If you have come through childhood with a true sense of Self, a well- formed self-identity, a sense of specialness, and the ability to love and to feel loveable, then, and only then, will relationships flow naturally. Relationship choices in people will be healthy. Relationships with other things, such as finances, religion, work, sexuality, etc., will be handled in fulfilling ways.

On the other hand, if you grew up with some or many of the dysfunctional family themes that were described in the previous chapters, and especially if you are fear-and shame based, then you, like many people, will have some or many struggles in life with relationships. This will continue until you become fully aware of what your wounds are, where they came from, and you are willing to face and to heal these wounds in Self.

So, how does this relate to the concept of co-dependency? Co-dependency, which is about an unfinished identity and the behaviors that develop from this as we adapt, develops out of family-of-origin dysfunctional relationships, which create distortions about Self. It is a mental disease, because it is out of sync with the normal flow of a human being. C-odependency is the disease we develop when we deny our true Self, while growing up in a dysfunctional family. Therefore, you end up in a dysfunctional and ineffective relationship with yourself.

To whatever degree you do not like yourself because of messages given and/or interpreted from parents, you will do or behave in the following ways:

1. Not treat yourself well and with respect. You may achieve a lot and acquire lots of material things, but you will find that this is no solution to Self-well-being. This can include not valuing and nurturing yourself physically, spiritually, mentally, and emotionally. You certainly will rarely listen to that little voice of your inner Self, who begs to be heard, if you even hear it at all

2. You will be afraid to take risks and make choices that might lead to success and that could enhance self-esteem, or you will take inappropriate risks.

3. You invariably will choose relationships that do not provide the nurture that you need but instead continue to reinforce your belief system that you are not good enough.

4. You will carry an inordinate amount of grief and anger toward those who instilled this negative belief system about yourself, and aware or not, you will displace these feelings onto other people.

5. You will be cheated of self-actualization, which is your birthright.

6. You will pass some or many versions of this co-dependency disease to your children, if you do not heal and claim your true Self. At the end of this chapter, I will list symptoms and styles of co-dependency."

Basically, when a child experiences enough of a dysfunctional, unsafe environment and behaviors by caretakers, he or she will, at least, mentally split off into two parts. There is, of course, our inner child, or true Self, about which much has been written. This first part of us is our essence of uniqueness, which we came in with as an infant. I believe our inner child contains our very soul, the only part of us that is spiritually connected and can truly love and connect with others. When things are hurtful and not safe, this part of us withdraws and hides away. What happens next, as the split occurs, is that this inner child becomes a wounded child, who in a sense is wrapped around our inner child and holds the secrets and hurts of the Self and of the family.

The wounded child is often very young. This part will remain frozen inside of us and requires lots of our energy to store and to defend these hurts, until we choose to go back and access it for emotional healing. These wounds will influence almost every choice we make, most importantly our choices of intimate relationships. Furthermore, these wounds will influence most of our other behaviors, will define our fears, and will get triggered like a raw sore when certain events and people come and go in our lives. This causes us to feel the pain of a particular stored wound and project it onto a different event or person, where it doesn't fit. This is a form of transference, which is the superimposing of feelings and/or reactions onto a person or event that actually belong to an earlier person or event. In these cases, we will make poor decisions, particularly with spouses and our children, because the wound is distorting our vision. This transference onto spouses and children is the major cause of conflict in couple-ships and abusive parenting.

To survive and protect the wounded child, we must find a way to defend Self and to live in this family by adapting. It often seems as if our true Self is a betrayal to our family, because it is rejected by them and doesn't meet their needs. Remember, in a healthy family, the parents are there for the children, but in a dysfunctional family, the children must be there for the parents. One of the more graphic ways in which this is reflected is when parents clearly see their children entirely as a reflection of themselves or expect the child to accomplish their unrequited dreams.

Therefore, we form an adaptive child, to protect this wounded inner child. This is the personality out of whom we then conduct most of our life. And, this is why I contend that we cannot just "get real" with only the aid of self-help books. It is always a child, often very young, who has formed this personality adaptive, and, therefore, is very ill-prepared for life as an adult, to make adult choices, and to choose healthy relationships. It is a defensive part of our personality. Remember that these splits and the roles we play in family of origin are not like roles in a play, where they later would be discarded. We continue to operate out of these early splits and roles long after we leave home. In fact, most people do this unknowingly for the rest of their lives.

RELATIONSHIP WITH SELF

This is the core of everything we do. Coming from dysfunctional homes, we generally do some degree of one of two things with our co-dependency, our unfulfilled needs, and our not fully formed identity: focus almost exclusively on everyone else, or focus almost exclusively on Self. Both are about survival, and both are dysfunctional. When you meet someone who seems to be self-centered, where everything is about them, it is really about them being stuck in survival mode stemming from family-of-origin trauma, with no ability to be outside of Self. Life for them is about vigilance, neediness, and fear. It's about trying to stay safe. Likewise, when you meet someone who is a constant caretaker of others, who seems to be selfless, or someone who meddles and tries to change and control others, this, too, is really about survival and fear. This comes from a need to control others to feel safe. These are two ways we get stuck while adapting for survival in our family of origin. Both are about trying to meet our needs. In a general sense, the one who focuses on others' needs has gotten stuck in this role out of some family theme, where they needed to become the parent and take care of other family members (the hero role). This is that person's attempt to stabilize the family system and to gain approval from the parents. The one who is very self-centered is often the one most blamed (the scapegoat role) and has been rejected or neglected in the family of origin. He/she is then left in a self-defensive role of trying to be okay with Self and to fit somewhere in this family's system.

What then happens to us in these roles? The caretaker constantly gives Self away, so therefore has a very rejecting relationship with

Self and carries a lot of anger about not getting his/her needs met by someone. The self-centered one has an aggrandized Self (false self-love) and continues behaviors in this role that cause rejection from others and isolates out of fear and low self-esteem, which keeps Self getting rejected and disliked. Obviously, the need is to free Self from these polarized positions, to learn to truly love and appreciate Self to create boundaries on giving, and to set boundaries on Self-only pursuits. This is, without a doubt, the most difficult part of recovery. We can change many outward behaviors and yet find these codependent themes are ever lurking in different masks. In dysfunctional families, there is lack of nurture and boundaries.

In my case, I took on the role of caregiver, fixer of problems, and superwoman at a very early age, but I also developed a good bit of self-centeredness as a result of being my mother's scapegoat of blame for everything that went wrong in the family. With a mother who was very negative, impossible to please, always finding something to be fearful of, and always finding fault, I countered by being optimistic, facing challenges with confidence (or so it appeared), and determined not to be like her. The problem was that I did this to prove her wrong and to solve her problems of fear. In the process, I swallowed my own fears and needs to be nurtured and reassured. In this way, I denied and rejected my Self.

My father was mostly absent, and it was not safe with him at times. I denied this, too, and built him up to be this fantasy hero, so that I had at least one good parent who I could believe loved me. This bad parent/good parent theme is very common with adult children and involves a lot of fantasy about both parents, especially about the good one. Here again, I sold myself out for his sake, repressed from my reality the memories of his unacceptable behavior when drunk, so that I could survive these disappointments and incongruities at a very young age. I did not know what my mother was going through with him, so I had no kind thoughts for her anger and mood swings. I learned after I grew up that she was trying to protect the family from the shame she experienced around his periodic drunk binges and was experiencing a lot of hurt and stress. Out of these early choices, which I had no awareness that I was making as a child, I set my path for much of my life. As I became an adult and married, I was destined to be the fixer again and a scapegoat for my husband, as I had been for my mother. I had married my mother, another person who could not look at their Self or acknowledge their flaws, another person to argue with defensively and endlessly.

We do, as part of the "stew," take on most of what our family of origin dishes out, one way or another. Sometimes, we are absolutely convinced that, "I am nothing like my mother, who was very critical." Then, low and behold, your children tell you, "You are critical, just like Grandma."

Part of what makes it so difficult to live our lives differently or to behave differently is that we are much like computers. We have been given the family input (both verbal and through behaviors), have stored it (much of it unknowingly), and then have grown up to spit it out, just like they did. One of the biggest ways we get tricked is by doing the opposite. Then, we think we are really different from them and better than they were. Amazingly, opposites generally come out the same way with same or similar results. For example, being critical and controlling of a child and ragging on him a lot, or, on the opposite end, ignoring a child by giving almost no input (so that he/she cannot decipher success or failure), both give the child poor self-esteem and lack of confidence. Either way, the child feels unimportant to those who mirror his/her value. And, from dysfunctional families, we learn very poor relationship skills, so that we are limited as parents to black-and-white or opposite responses, such as either using heavy abusive discipline or no discipline at all. There are no gray areas or in-betweens, which are things we would learn in a healthy family.

Again, we are profoundly affected by how we are related to from the very beginning. Self soaks up what is around it like a sponge, positive or negative. There are no defenses. Self begins forming a self-concept of being valuable or not.

We cannot ask a very small child to formulate their experiences. Many events and their impacts from very early childhood are not cognitively remembered, and a child will protect parents first (not tell bad things about them), so we can mostly only recognize what happened to us very early on by our eventual adult behaviors and symptoms. This is especially hard where there has been sexual abuse that is not cognitively remembered, because the wound inside is frozen or repressed, as a result of fear at a very young age. Also, children especially are inclined to protect the parent, or not want to know or to remember this kind of thing. Yet, the symptoms are in their adult life.

What happens to Self in childhood is assumed to be the norm by most children. Therefore, if there is a theme of addiction in the family, such as alcoholism or a lot of drinking and partying, children assume this is how all families function. The Self has lived in this theme of alcoholism, so it has no internal meter to measure what is healthy drinking. It often is said that children of alcoholics are the last people to be able to recognize alcoholism, no matter how severe, because it was normalized in the family.

If dad is distant or angry a lot, instilling fear in the family, children may assume all fathers/men are like this. If this is a boy child, then he may be looking at Self in a negative way, perhaps deciding that men, one of whom he will become, are not nice people.

Someone I know told a story of how her son, after listening to her frequently make deprecating remarks about men, looked at her and said: "Mom, since I am a boy, do you feel those awful things about me?" The woman shared that she was horrified and hadn't realized how this impacted her little boy. She immediately stopped the remarks. She had generalized and transferred her childhood experiences with men and subsequent choices in relationships with men to form her belief about all men. Of course, it bears repeating that she, like many people, did not realize that she had chosen, as a result of her childhood wounds, only men who would replicate the men who had wounded her and made negative impacts. Therefore, her relationships with men as an adult further reinforced her early beliefs about men, because she continued to have negative experiences. We choose relationships this way because of unfinished business and our wounds from childhood relationships. We are looking to solve, change, and heal ourselves by unconsciously choosing people who are similar to those with whom we had negative childhood experiences. She was lucky that her son told her how this was affecting his Self- perception. Most children would not share but would just internalize the messages to Self.

If mom is a people pleaser, always giving Self away, then a female child may decide that a girl has no worth compared to men and follow in mom's footsteps. This, of course, also has historical roots of women being viewed as inferior. These are negative lessons learned about ones' gender from the modeling of a particular parent.

Family beliefs and deeply held attitudes in a dysfunctional, closed family system essentially are force-fed to the children. Marilyn vos Savant, once wrote in response to a reader question in her weekly article in Parade magazine that she did not think attitudes could be changed, because they are so deeply ingrained in the individual. These beliefs and attitudes, which we are force-fed in our family of origin, can be about life in general, the nature of the world, who you can trust, who are not "our kind of people," religion, money, etc. From my experiences as a therapist, I believe they are naturally adopted and deeply held by very young children, who have no access to other views. But, I believe they can be changed with intrapersonal work, particularly the kind that is done in a group. People who join, for example, the Ku Klux Klan, an organization based on hate, were not born believing that certain other people are bad because of race or color. They were carefully taught these ideas by their families or perhaps by not feeling loved or important in their families. Thus, they were vulnerable to join a cult like this, which could make them feel special, important, and chosen. We all need to feel special and chosen to value Self.

Naturally, our beliefs and attitudes either help us to connect in positive ways in our relationships with people, places, and things, or they impede us from being able to connect effectively and flow naturally in the world. There are religious groups that draw their members from this kind of vulnerability, where people need to feel special and chosen.

Finally, there is the input to Self about Self, as seen and experienced from parents, caretakers, other family members, teachers, babysitters, and others. If the input is positive in the early years of a child and the modeling of these important people is congruent with what they say and teach, then you can expect to grow up with good self-esteem. You cannot expect a child to believe they are wonderful and loveable if parents model giving themselves away, putting themselves down verbally (teaching, for example, that "we are always full of sin"), and/or being abusive. Then, it will be very hard to have good self-esteem as life goes on.

In dysfunctional families, however, the Self does not get loaded up with good messages about the Self. At worst, there is a lot of verbal abuse, cutting the child down emotionally. Then, there is "crazy making," where there are lots of mixed messages and one does not know what to believe about how they view you or feel about you. Finally, there are subtle messages in body language, voice tone, and implied messages that you are not quite living up to their expectations. And, physical or sexual abuse includes a very deprecating message in the act itself, whether verbalized or not. These contribute to building a negative relationship with Self. One then grows up with a fragile self-concept. How fragile this is depends on how dysfunctional the family-of-origin relationships were.

There are a lot of tragedies that result from a poor sense of Self and lack of self-esteem/self-love. (By the way, some teachings have muddled up the idea of self- love, confusing it with selfishness). When parents, family, and others shower love onto a child, the child is — and is supposed to be — learning to love Self. This does not mean they give the child everything he/she wants or that they do not set boundaries. Also, they are clear to make corrective messages about behavior, not about character/identity. Without love of Self, you cannot give intimate love to another, and you will choose relationships that do not give love to the Self. This perpetuates a cycle of reinforcing the belief that Self is not loveable, and then self-esteem heads in an ever downward cycle. Relationships are chosen or handled in ways that continue to tear at self-esteem, rather than build it up. If one feels unworthy and unloveable, then how can he/she be entitled to success and happiness? There will be failed personal relationships, failed businesses, lack of money, and an inherent feeling of powerlessness and worthlessness.

Human beings are profound survivors, even as little children, so we find ways to survive some of the worst traumas and family conditions. How we do this is by mentally/emotionally splitting off. Rather than getting into heavy clinical definitions, I prefer to refer to this as forming parts of our personality. In extreme cases of abuse, children make these splits deeper, with the ability to disassociate, and in some cases form what are called multiple personalities. These concepts of splits in the personality are very helpful in looking at how we are able to survive trauma. As I said before, we are not stamped out of cookie cutters. As much as there are many similarities in process, experiences, and ways in which we operate as individuals, there still will be broad differences in how we form these parts of ourselves as we adapt. In psychology, especially in the addictions field, which turned the concept of dysfunctional family into a household word, there has been much written about the roles children take on in dysfunctional families.

I have known and worked with people, who have said they like/love their Self, yet, as we explored further, it became clear that their life theme and behaviors reflected just the opposite. They had often substituted grandiosity for self-esteem. They are unsuccessful in relationships, or do not take care of themselves physically, mentally, or spiritually, or always put others' needs before their own, or all of the above. In all areas of life, remember that if the behavior does not match the words, it is the behavior that tells the truth. We can form many false and incongruent ideas about ourselves without realizing it, but our behavior will reflect our true beliefs. My hope is that some or several of my chapters will bring light to the reader's symptoms and stuck places. Hopefully, the reader will be able to recognize where behaviors come from that aren't working effectively, ,or in a fulfilling way. Most of all, I hope this book will help the reader on a path to find the real Self.

Relationship with Self Questionnaire

1. Do you recognize that you do not have good self-esteem when looking at how you treat yourself in your daily living? If so, what are some of the ways in which you are unkind to yourself or put yourself last?
2. Do you abuse food, drugs, or money, and tell yourself that it is a way of being good to yourself?
3. Do you clearly know your beliefs and attitudes and where they originated? Define them for yourself, noting prejudices about others and about your feeling toward others' differences. How are your feelings the same or different from your parents or other original primary caretakers?
4. Do you recognize yourself in the dysfunctional family roles, as have been described so far?
5. Do you believe that you are shame based and/or have an inordinate amount of fear?
6. Do you get extremely angry with yourself when you make a mistake or do not do something perfectly?
7. How do you feel about yourself? What messages do you give yourself when you succeed at something? And when you make a mistake or feel you have failed at something?
8. Are you critical of others? Of Self? Do you say derogatory things in your head about yourself?
9. Did you grow up in a family who practiced a particular religion?
10. How has religion influenced your life? Do you practice it today? Have you done research on religions or spiritual paths

Symptoms and Styles of Co-dependency

- Never or rarely feeling comfortable around other people.
- An underlying basic feeling of not being good enough.
- Giving yourself away and going along with things with which you do not agree.
- Preoccupation with rescuing others and putting Self last.
- Compulsion to be in charge and do it all yourself.
- Trying to control/CHANGE other people and going to great lengths to make your point heard. Example: Giving self-help books to friends and family, or continuing to argue on and on and being inflexible in your views.
- Bringing up the past over and over.
- Avoiding confrontation and anger at all costs or using anger to control others.
- Having a feeling of guilt if you choose yourself or something for yourself over someone else's wishes or needs, as you see them, or fantasize that they are.
- Having to be right and building a stockpile of resentments when this is not acknowledged.
- Having a great deal of trouble letting go of other people's behavior, obsessing with anger and righteousness. Seeking or obsessing about getting revenge.
- Unforgiving of Self and often of others, like in stockpiling grudges.
- Terrified you will forget something or make a mistake, fear driven.
- Never satisfied with Self; no achievement is enough. There is always a new goal.
- Tired a lot but compulsed to over schedule your life.

- Unable to appreciate your successes or take in (to Self) compliments and affirmations.
- Extremely critical of Self.
- Feeling hopeless about repetitive failed relationships or about being stuck in the current one, and going through the same painful arguments over and over.
- Making choices over and over that ignore that little voice in you that says, "Don't do this; it doesn't work."
- Believing that parents or anyone who you admire or who become significant to you have all or better answers than you, OR believing that YOU have, or should have, all the answers.
- Feeding/medicating your empty feelings and wounds with alcohol, drugs, food, nicotine, shopping, sex, fantasy, or relationship obsession.
- Critical of others, biased and/or threatened by differences such as race, culture, and sexual orientation of others.

CHAPTER FOURTEEN

RELATIONSHIP WITH MONEY

Is is addictive? What causes Greed? Is it my friend?

As adaptive children, most of us try to manage money with the limited skills of a child, using private logic, and making decisions that are the result of our primary caretaker's inability to properly manage money. That's all we know.

Most people don't stop to realize just how powerful and pervasive a role in our entire life the management or mismanagement of our money plays. The organization and flow of life are greatly determined by how finances are handled and by whether there is order or chaos. Money issues, usually about fear of lack, can be such a central focus in a family that all life seems to revolve around it. Today it is a dysfunctional world focus!! The relationship to money of the Republican party is so transparent, and something that is quite frightening when we imagine the harm it can do to all of us. There is more about this in Chapter 20, the new addition to this book.

Certainly, people don't think of having a dysfunctional relationship with money. The meaning of this is a disorder of the mental health and lack of skills handling finances. Unfortunately, it is ALWAYS fallout from one's family of origin, for this is where we form our original relationship with money. As children, we form our private logic around things we don't fully understand and end up with further distortions. Few children are taught how to have a healthy relationship with money. Instead, in dysfunctional families, money is usually fraught with anger, power struggles, withholding, crazy-making, and unfairness.

Money, or the lust for it, and/or mismanagement of it, also has the power to hurt, destroy, and take away all of our rights. We are experiencing global mismanagement of finances, making it easy to recognize the profound role that money plays in everyone's life!

We often see evidence of this in how the wealthy and powerful have destroyed stability in our financial world. Examples of this are the scandals of Enron, AIG, and Madoff. This is due to their dishonest relationship with money, mismanagement, and greed. A great percentage of crime is about getting more money or material things. Often, too, it is about resentment of those who have more money. Money has been called "the root of all evil."

On a less grand level, many of those who are financially disordered experience the necessity of bankruptcy (a very shaming process) or years of deprivation from running up insurmountable debts which they are trying to pay off to avoid bankruptcy. Many face years of poor credit ratings, which is also very shaming and creates more deprivation. Thus, a healthy relationship with money is a critical part of good self-esteem and a fulfilling life.

Many people are still caught in a child's magical thinking regarding money. I often have heard a client say, "Oh, the money always comes from somewhere." This is magical thinking! In fact, where the money comes from will be, in a sense, stolen or borrowed from another owner. By owner, I mean that this money belongs, or is promised to, the home mortgage company, electric company, phone company, credit card company, or some other person or institution that you have promised to pay when due. The money also might be borrowed by delaying a promised repayment to a relative or friend. These alternatives to the "money always coming from somewhere" complicate the situation even more, as now there is a future need for more money and more OWNERS OF YOUR MONEY to repay. There also will be more need to manipulate your resources, as you spiral further into debt.

Borrowing from relatives and friends can bring other complications, such as rationalizing that they can wait (forever possibly) and, therefore, creating bad feelings, avoidance of contact, and internal shame. Borrowing from credit cards creates more debt. In fact, this process of magical thinking, while actually "robbing Peter to pay Paul" is an addictive thinking pattern, using the unconscious philosophy of "I'll quit tomorrow," meaning I'll catch up tomorrow.

Another highly dysfunctional process in the relationship with money is floating checks or postdating checks, meaning a check is written and given or mailed before the money is in the bank to cover it. This is a form of gambling, as you are risking that your paycheck will come in exactly on time, that you are not out sick that day (or other emergency that delays the banking of it), and that the bank will not hold it too long. If these checks bounce, then bank fees render you further in debt, leaving you with even less choices for spending.

Another very prevalent issue with adult children from dysfunctional homes is spending or paying without keeping an accurate balance in the checkbook. Many call the bank every day to see what their current balance is, as if there are no additional checks written that would hold a claim on the account. This is like Russian roulette, and another form of magical thinking, which allows one to spend money that doesn't exist or no longer belongs to you. Other forms of magical thinking and gambling are chronic buying of lotto tickets, investments in get-rich-quick schemes, and pyramid deals.

The drive or compulsive need to look good or always have the best, creates a lot of dysfunctional spending and over-spending of money. Many buy homes, cars, clothes, and luxuries they cannot afford to look good on the outside. More than one client has shared that even though his family struggled to make ends meet, they dressed impeccably when attending church or other public events, where they would be seen by others. At home, the parents would waste money on non-necessities and not provide things the children needed.

Some children grow up with an AVOIDANT style with money. This will mean avoiding bills by not going to the mailbox, putting bills away unopened and ignoring them, and avoiding people or situations where they owe money. The avoidant style is based in fear and creates more fear in the process (self-fulfilling prophesy). Others may just try to avoid money.

Blanche didn't know why she was so afraid to have or keep any money. Her adult family was constantly in money crisis, and there were constant crises paying bills. As soon as she felt caught up, there would be another family accident or illness, or she would get injured, so that work for income was missed, creating more anxiety around money. Sometimes, she would just lose large sums of cash. When reading some of my materials about telationship with money, she was surprised to remember her parents often fought about money. She had been so distressed by this fighting, that she unconsciously had made a childhood decision that she would never let money mean anything to her. As a result, she had spent much of her adult life avoiding money by losing it or spending it unwisely. She actually felt a lot of anxiety if there was extra money. Her childhood decision created a self-fulfilling prophesy, in that there has been negativity and anxiety surrounding money all of her life, because she doesn't manage it in a healthy manner. She came to realize that it was not the money that was a problem; it was that her parents didn't know how to manage money, and exhibited anger and fear around it. This "lack of" has been a theme in her own family, and the entire family process has been centered around chaos, crisis, no budget, and not enough earning of income by her or her husband. Since the children have grown and have good jobs, Blanche has become dependent on them for constant bailouts.

Parents, who provide too much money and material things in place of love, attention, and emotional support, can create a child who grows up unable to go out and achieve financial success. Sometimes, this is about wanting the parent to pay (because money is love in this family), or it can be the result of being allowed to be too dependent. This creates low self-esteem around earning and managing money. This also can create over-entitlement or under-entitlement in a child. In both cases, the child will grow up with unhealthy thinking and a lack of ability to earn enough or to manage money. In families where money is love, there is often much conflict and hurt around inheritance.

Compulsive spending is a key dysfunction for most adult children. It is a way in which we often try to medicate feelings, like using alcohol or other drugs, sex, or food. It requires rationalizing and magical thinking, if we overspend our budget. Compulsive spending is mostly about trying to fill the emotional void within the proverbial hole in the soul. Many times it involves having clothes in the closet that still have the tags on them, or toys and electronics that are never used.

The fallout of a dysfunctional relationship with money is severe in couple-ship. Often, there are two people with different versions of money dysfunction. One person may be over-entitled, while the other is under-entitled, which creates more deprivation for the under-entitled. One may be a hoarder, while the other is overly generous, or an over-spender. Clashes will occur over control of money. Children witness these conflicts and begin to form their fears and unhealthy decisions about the meaning of money. When there is divorce, money is very often a major area of conflict. One partner may clean out the savings account or refuse to pay child support. On the other hand, one partner may stubbornly say they need nothing from the other, even when they will be the custodial parent. The children's needs often are forgotten in the battle between partners.

Ending up with a dysfunctional relationship with money is a very common outcome of growing up in a family with addictions or other dysfunctions. It also is an outcome of living in a country and a society that fosters unhealthy money relationships. We usually end up REACTING to money, rather than learning to use it as a tool to enhance our lives.

Bill grew up in a severely dysfunctional family, where there was drug addiction, leading to his mother going to jail, and divorce, leading to his having no connection to his dad from age five until twelve. At times, he was living in poverty, experiencing many abandonments, and pervasive sexual abuse and incest. As an adult, when Bill explored his family history, he learned that his father suffered a severe trauma at age sixteen, which clearly arrested his emotional development and later manifested into his attraction to young boys. As a result, when Bill visited him in his teen years there was a role reversal, with Bill advising, rescuing, and trying to help his father become financially successful in business. In every instance, Bill was dumped on by his father and not rewarded financially for his efforts. These were situations where a son might expect a father, who had been absent while he was a child, to grab an opportunity to be there for him. Instead, his father would take care of other young boys, who he rescued financially, while never hiding this from Bill. Bill so badly wanted to have at least one caring and responsible parent, so he held onto the fantasy of his father being a good guy, who would rescue him someday. In reality, Bill's father was irresponsible with money (made and inherited a lot, and lost it over and over) and was very self-centered. Bill stayed in this role-reversal relationship into his thirties, hanging onto a childhood fantasy of his father. As a result, Bill has been confused about money as an adult, had periods of making a lot of money and then blowing it, and has many control issues regarding money. These dysfunctional money issues played a major role in his addiction process, the failing of his marriage, and difficulty maintaining other relationships.

Deprivation creates the overspending of money, at least periodically, which in turn creates more deprivation. It then becomes a vicious cycle. For example, there can be excessive overspending for holidays, such as Christmas, or occasions such as weddings, which creates future debt and the inability to provide necessities. Very few, if any, dysfunctional families have a budget or handle money responsibly. The area of creating a budget is a very important aspect of the healing work with the addictive population. Budgeting sets boundaries. Boundaries are something that addicts and family members of addicts do not have. Wealthy adult children often have these money dysfunctions, but they do not show up as much as those in a lower-income family. If nothing else, these children will use wealth as control and power.

Hoarding is often another outcome of money deprivation from childhood. This does not necessarily only apply to money itself, but also includes such things as food, clothes, and supplies. An example is storing the best towels or dishes and using the older ones. Many people, who went through the 1930s Great Depression, became hoarders out of fear of having another financial trauma. As a result of experiencing trauma, children and adults make extreme decisions, conscious and unconscious, to avoid recurrence of that trauma.

There are many stories of dysfunctional money addictions that I have heard over the years. My own story involved growing up with parents who had formed their money compulsions from the same trauma. Both, having grown up in families where there was poverty during the Depression, adapted in opposite ways. We were never poor or wanting, and by the time I was ten, we lived in an upper-middle-class home and neighborhood. We had two cars, and I could usually get most of what I wanted, especially by manipulating my father. My mother was extremely fear-based about money and worried about it all the time, hoarding it, along with extra food and supplies. Everything for her was first viewed in terms of how much it would cost. Her anxiety and negativity around this permeated my acquiring of things. This was especially sad, for example, when I made the cheerleading team, and her first response was, "What will this cost?" Mother was seen by relatives and me, as being very selfish, because we did not understand the roots of her hoarding. Though we had plenty, she once charged a poor relative, who had many children, a quarter for a baby blanket. This was very embarrassing and of course, affected her relationship with the relatives in a negative way.

My father, on the other hand, would never set limits on my expenditures, which caused friction between him and my mother, made her look more selfish, and made her view me even more negatively. He was a workaholic, but, as is the case with addiction, nothing was enough. He could never make Mother feel secure, even though he was very successful. My father was a lost child, loaded with guilt about his alcoholism and sex addiction, especially coming from a religious, fundamentalist family. As an adult child, I chose my father as my money mentor. I was an over spender and did not learn the value of money and taking care of myself in this area until I was in my forties. I was also a workaholic (until 25 years ago), and spent all the money I earned. This constantly created money anxiety for me. It's interesting that by not saving, an extreme reaction to my mother, who saved everything, I had no financial security should I become unable to work. My addictive relationship with money was created by my relationship with my parents.

Don grew up in a poor family. There was never extra money for anything beyond the barest essentials. His father turned a blind eye to the finances, while his mother tried to manage the money. Periodically, she would remark to the children that she had gone shopping and bought things they couldn't afford, but told them to keep it a secret from Dad. Quite often, the children would hear the parents arguing about money. One day, his little six-year-old brother told his mother, while riding in the car, that he needed to go to the dollar store. He came back with a package of fake money and told her, "Now, you don't have to worry about money anymore." This Don remembers as evidence of how much money anxiety was in his family.

In Don's first marriage, he relegated the money management to his wife, following the example of his parents, probably because he had emotionally divorced himself from his childhood negative feelings regarding money. Even though it didn't work, it replicated what was done by his parents. Sure enough, as could be predicted, his wife overspent the money. Though there was plenty between their two merged incomes, there was no money when he wanted to get something special — and he had learned as a child not to want much. He was traumatized again. Therefore, he now had a double trauma around money and females, and made a promise to himself that no one would ever spend his money again. He resolved never to feel financially insecure again!

Several years later when he married again, Don made it clear that he and his new wife would each have their own money. His second wife had her dysfunctional reasons for accepting this, because she also came from a money-deprived family of origin, and as a result, wanted to spend her own money. She had a history of magical thinking in regard to money and had been previously married to a man who was a hoarder and didn't want to spend money on anything except necessities. She came to the second marriage with a lot of anger about this and the deprivations as a child. Their problems began when he retired and was on Social Security and a pension. She also had developed a medically expensive illness. He became more possessive of his money. Then, they began to have money- struggle issues. She wanted to spend more on things for the home and traveling (afraid her illness would be terminal), and for him to be less thrifty. It pained him to see how she wanted to spend money on replacing anything that still served its function, regardless of how old or outdated, or to spend money on traveling abroad. He didn't need anything and felt she was wasteful. He worried about taking care of them in the future. They had opposite opinions, and money became more and more of an issue. In therapy, it became necessary to help them look at their childhood money wounds. It is easy to see how one's relationship with money can permeate and start to destroy the more important relationship with spouse, like what happens when there is alcohol and drug addiction.

A dysfunctional relationship with money creates a lot of anxiety. It very much impacts our relationships in many ways and our choices. Making it even more complicated is that we live in a society that worships money and things. Thus, it is so very easy to feel deprived and make poor money choices. And, as we all know we are living in a money dysfunctional system. It is dominating our government as it is our personal choices.

Relationship with Money Questionnaire

Is it addictive? What causes Greed? How does it affect your other relationships?

1. How do you relate to money?
2. How did your family relate to/handle money? Who managed it?
3. Have you experienced money deprivation? Overindulgence?
4. Were your parents deprived or overindulged?
5. Did your parents quarrel over money and how it was spent? Blame?
6. Did either parent hoard money or things bought with it?
7. Specifically, how has your money management effected your life?

Chapter Fifteen

RELATIONSHIP WITH DENIAL

How We Can Overload with this Defense Mechanism

I am placing this chapter here, between Relationship with Money, and Relationship with Addictions, as I believe money and addiction are the clearest areas in which to learn about our denial.

Denial is an innate ability that enables us at any given time to alter our perception of reality when it is unacceptable to our psyche. We do this by using methods of avoidance, such as repression to push it out of our memory and into the unconscious, projection to blame someone else, rationalization to form an explanation that has just enough truth in it to almost make sense, and/or minimization, declaring to Self that "It wasn't that bad." I call these reactive behaviors the "soldiers of denial:" repression, rationalization, projection, and minimization. Repression is the most protective, because it stores memories in the unconscious. If an individual wishes to access these memories, it almost always requires the aid of psychotherapy. This is because a lot of trust, guidance, and support are required to walk back into these memories. However, the payoffs in healing relationships can be worth the required time and effort.

On the positive side, denial has great value in preserving our sanity by preventing an intolerable overload of emotions from major traumatic experiences, such as the sudden loss of a loved one. It preserves us when traumas need to be absorbed more slowly, or not experienced, such as when we repress them. Denial allows the reality to seep in at a slower pace. This is the way the grieving process works, which is a healthy defense mechanism. It also allows us to tolerate living in the unsure and often unsafe reality of the world at large, to age without constant fear of death, and to stay functional even when someone we love is in great danger (over which we have no control) or is very ill or dying from disease. Somehow, we persevere with hope, though we often realize later that this was not in reality. It allows people to go to war and to fight on the front lines by not fixating on how much danger they are in, how close to death they are, or what they actually are doing to other humans.

Denial is a very important defense mechanism. However, our relationship with denial can permeate our relationships in very destructive ways throughout our life, depending on how much we may have had to overuse it as a child. Our denial, like even our good qualities, sometimes can be our nemesis, especially when we try to gain more awareness of Self and to clear our psyche, so that we can be open to more of the world than we could while growing up. This is often due to the adapting that we have had to do to survive growing up. In this case, our internal locker of stored wounds is being jealously guarded by a big strong soldier called Denial. This also is because stored wounds live in an internalized small-child part of us, which I refer to as our wounded child. These wounds are frozen in memories and fears that occurred when they were more than a child could handle. All of the denial that we internally have constructed to guard these wounds will permeate our relationships, until the wounds are opened and healed. These childhood traumas, which are frozen and fear-based, create phobias, such as fear of closed spaces, heights, insects, leaving the house, and many more.

Denial, when used as it was intended, to protect the psyche, is a healthy defense mechanism, which we need. However, when we linger in denial, we develop a dysfunctional relationship with it, which will intrude on our relationships in ways that are not healthy. For example, a dysfunctional family, such as one with alcoholism, takes on the addiction disease by becoming what we call co-dependent and employing its behaviors, because they don't want the problem to be reality. The fallout from this as an adult is that we transfer this denial into other situations, especially with relationships that are important to us. We try to avoid reality, when it will cause us pain or loss. Thus, like in the alcoholic family, we will try to change the person who is or has the problem, rather than accept it is a problem that we cannot control.

Denial is different from lying, because it is not a purposeful conscious method to deceive others. The Self is deceived first and believes the newly formed reality. It is very much a part of how children in dysfunctional homes survive abuse and abandonment, by adapting to form a new reality about their parents, for example. In these cases, children either minimize their pain ("It wasn't that bad"), project by blaming the parent's behavior on one of their siblings or the other parent, or rationalize ("Dad is just under stress"). Children sometimes simply deny to themselves that it affected them and carry deep wounds of anger and hurt, which get displaced onto other people. They learn to understand in their head, stuffing their feelings.

Denial is about fear. The more dysfunction in a child's home, the more denial will play a part in his/her adult life. Choices in lifestyle, partners, friends, careers, and religious affiliations will be dictated by this major defense mechanism. Closed family and religious systems create fear of new ideas, of gaining broader knowledge. These closed systems create fear, and fear creates the inability to grow and to change.

Understanding denial becomes particularly important in the understanding and treatment of addiction. Quite simply, denial allows one to stay in and sink deeper into the disease of addiction, without seeing it in reality. For example, the addicted person, such as an alcoholic, little by little, month by month, changes reality in his/her own head, so that the addictive use or behavior can still continue. This process protects the addiction, rather than the psyche, and actually leads to more pain and problems. You no doubt are familiar with many famous and wealthy people, such as some of our top actors, who seem to have everything, yet throw their lives away on drugs and alcohol. How can this happen? Don't they see what is happening? The answer is no, they do not! Powerful, bright, beautiful people regularly throw their lives away in the disease of addiction. Without the defense mechanism of denial, this could never happen. It allows us to change our reality. This is how we best can explain that addiction is a mental disease.

Although the destructive use of denial can be more easily seen when you understand how it works with addiction, the truth is that all of us who grew up in dysfunctional families have inherited a significant dose of denial. Also, we had to use denial to survive things such as family dynamics, described in Chapters 2, 3, and 4. When growing up in a family with one or many versions of these dynamics, one needs a significant amount of denial and becomes well practiced at using it.

The process of adapting creates co-dependency, which is defined here as an incomplete identity formation because of lack of enough safety, enough nurture, and healthy boundaries in the home environment. It causes children to adapt to the family, rather than to develop Self. Thus, we become codependent in our behaviors as children, adapting as best we can and using denial to protect our young minds from what we don't understand and don't want to be true. We learn to make up a reality that makes us feel a little safer and more secure, along with made-up answers for what we do not understand. We call this private logic. This way of thinking does not go away as we grow up.

My purpose in discussing denial in depth is so that the reader may understand that digesting this book may be difficult at times. Most of us have our buried wounds, which enable us to have some pretty heavy denial defenses that make us scared to dig for answers. I want to emphasize that although you may have buried pain, you also have a real buried treasure of SELF.

My hope is that this discussion will encourage you to take in this book one chapter at a time, dealing with one concept at a time. Chapters 2, 3, and 4 include a lot of possibilities and can help you open doors to your history and understand how that combines to make you who you are today. Most of all, you will learn how your family history relates to your interactions in relationships. If you want to get the most out of this material or find it especially overwhelming, I cannot overemphasize the value of working with a therapist who specializes in family-of-origin issues and who can help you break through denial.

Questionnaire on Relationship with Denial

How we can overload with this defense
mechanism that we all have

1. Can you distinguish between denial and lying?
2. Have you ever realized that you have been in denial about something in particular? Explain.
3. Have you observed someone else's denial after they lost someone to death?
4. Have you thought that someone you have known to be alcoholic/drug addicted was lying, rather than in denial?
5. Are you aware of defense mechanisms you may have, such as minimizing, rationalizing, or projecting, that may support your denial?
6. Do you believe it is possible that you may have repressed some memories, because the incidents were too painful to handle?
7. Can you connect the process of denial in your process of money relationship and/or in your thinking about addiction?

CHAPTER SIXTEEN

RELATIONSHIP WITH ADDICTION

Food, Alcohol, Drugs, Money, Work, Religion, Sex, and Love Relationships

I have specialized for thirty years in helping people get into recovery from substance and compulsive behavior addictions. I am not exaggerating when I say that addictions are epidemic in our country. Most people do not recognize, in particular, the stages of addiction and the functional stages of the disease. In addition, only alcohol and other drugs are widely recognized as relevant to the term addiction. When you add sex, food, Internet, relationships, and money-related addictions, such as shopping, gambling, overspending, and hoarding, to the addiction criteria, it is easier to see the wide scope of the addictive process and especially how it prevents emotional intimacy. The addiction is always the first priority and first love, in the addict's life.

In addition, when it comes to defining addiction, I believe most people do not recognize that everything we do involves the brain. Thus, there is much difficulty in understanding that addiction is a mental disease, which activates and underlies drug/alcohol use. My favorite definition of addiction is one coined by a priest, Father Martin, who many years ago made a film, "Chalk Talk," which was shown for years to recovering addicts in treatment centers. He simplified it to: "If it's a problem, it's a problem." And, it always is. Addiction, to anything, supersedes personal relationships and continues despite the problems it creates. The addicted brain is the driving force. Physical addiction creates craving, but many people in various stages of addiction do not become physically addicted, but are, in fact, very addicted. Craving also comes from emotional pain, which sends messages requesting the need to medicate/block out painful feelings. The brain sends behavioral messages and rationalizations to the person, making it okay to medicate. This is the disease.

We are a society/world in the midst of phenomenal changes. People, especially those who do not have good self-esteem and solid stability, do not like change. I am sad to say that a huge percentage of us are, or have been, in this category. In addition, we are connected to and vulnerable to most of the world through our phenomenal technological advances. We are running scared, no doubt as much or more as was the case during the Great Depression and World War II. Thus, we medicate our fears in many ways, with many drugs and behaviors unknown seventy years ago, during those hard times. Sadly, this makes us not very emotionally available in relationships.

And, because there is immense distrust of differences, especially in religion and race we still haven't gotten beyond centuries of warfare. We live in fear of being attacked and possibly annihilated on any given day. The need to medicate is therefore much more intense than in times past, when we felt less globally vulnerable and much safer. An example of this is the tremendous increase in obesity, which is rooted in the addiction process and is not just about eating more fast food but is about eating more food in order to anesthetize ourselves.

One of the most amazing and sad facts is that physicians are not trained to recognize, treat, and/or refer addicted patients. They receive about one and one half hours of didactic lectures in this area! Physicians have the greatest possibility to refer patients for help. The only referral I received was an alcoholic woman with late-stage liver disease. This, of course, only when her condition was so severe that it was hard to ignore. Physicians could be great leaders, interventionists, life savers, and facilitators of prevention. In not doing so, they are enablers of the disease.

Now, to look at the etiology of addiction on an individual level, we need to look at how one's relationship with addiction develops. This, of course, takes us again to our "family stew," from whence we came. Each of us have our own reactions in our family of origin, and there are differences in how we adapt even from the same family. We develop roles to get our needs met or simply to survive in the more severe dysfunctional relationships and environments. However, one cannot grow up in a family, where there is addiction, without developing some form of this family disease. This is because addiction in the family, be it parent(s) or grandparent(s), siblings, or other close relative, creates emotional wounds in the child, because it is not safe, not predictable or consistent, creates fear, and requires adapting. Children growing up with addiction in the family adapt, learn to medicate, or use a different way of medicating, such as compulsive behavioral addictions. In short, they have adapted to the family dysfunction and will be attracted to relationships that are similar, along with no understanding of the nature of addiction and how it happens.

Addiction is something that most of us are vulnerable to because of our fear and wounds. Once we have adopted the addictive process, it encompasses our entire being, physically, mentally, emotionally, and spiritually. It is our most available way

-— and effective for a period of time — to avoid emotional pain. As addiction progresses, it becomes our most important ally, and we will protect and defend our connection to it, above all else, even as it increases pain and becomes a negative, self-destructive ally.

First of all, when one is in relationship with addiction, it is a great obstruction to intimacy. Addictions involve a planning to connect with the drug or behavioral compulsion, such as gambling, scheduling other things around it, so that one can get the fix. Sneaking, hiding evidence, a sense of excitement at the anticipation, and the over-use of the substance or behavioral compulsion are part of the addictive process. Denial plays a very in-depth and important role in addictions. This ability to form our own truth includes the very useful tools of rationalization, minimization, and projection (blaming). The experience of blackouts, usually with chemical addictions but sometimes with rage, adds to the addict's ability to be out of touch with reality. Also, sometimes there is lying — anything to protect one's stash and/or ability to continue using the substance or compulsion. However, do not assume that denial and lying are the same thing, as I explained in the earlier chapter on Denial. Shame, of course, is also a big factor in an addict's need to be dishonest, as addicts feel like failures when it comes to controlling their addiction, which cannot be done. Internal shame increases as the addiction progresses, but the addict often will exhibit grandiosity externally.

When we are born into a family where our caretakers are addicted, we already have a strike against us in terms of falling into this disease ourselves. It is medically known that alcoholics have a physiological predisposition from family of origin and ancestry. Add to this the emotional abuse and often physical and/or sexual abuse in an alcoholic or other addicted family. We are destined to have emotional and psychological wounds, which add to our probability of medicating our pain with substances or compulsions. Also, added to this is the modeling of addictive behaviors and use of medicators by our parents or other caretakers. With all this input, what are our chances of escaping falling into the addictive process? And, with all this input, we already have a relationship with addiction! We likely will either become addicts, or choose relationships (spouses/partners/ friendships) with others who are addicts or who are from addictive families — or both. Even though we do not consciously wish for it, we are attracted to what is familiar.

Most of us, as children of alcoholics or other drug addicts, only recognize addiction in the style of our family of origin. That usually means we do not recognize other addictions or its stages. Also, addiction often is treated as a normal part of the family process. This is why we call it a family disease. This means that children of these families do not recognize that they, too, are addicted, because their drug of choice is different from that of their parent(s) or other caretaker(s). Or, many say that they will not get out of control with it, as their parents did. Examples of this are use of pot instead of alcohol; food addiction, such as overeating, bulimia, anorexia; gambling; overspending and many other forms of money addiction; sex addiction, (which is hard to acknowledge because of shame); love addiction; and work addiction. For example, it is easy to believe you have escaped being an addict "like Mom," who is on prescribed drugs, because your drug of choice is different or does not have the same visible impact, as alcohol or other drugs. The truth is that addictions not only have an impact on the addict, but also deeply affect others around them.

An addiction that still is not seen seriously enough is nicotine. Even though the Surgeon General compared it to cocaine addiction several years ago, and even though there is massive evidence of how deadly nicotine is, we still do not recognize it as we do other drugs. There is not a lot of help for the addiction. I am not referring to pills and cures that are advertised but to the need for emotional help in stopping smoking.

Eating disorders, for example, such as are inherent in obesity and anorexia, greatly impact self-esteem and health. It affects children in the family where there is an obese parent. Also, it affects parents when children become obese or anorexic to avoid being fat. Remember, children think and choose in the black-and-white, either/or mode, so a middle road, such as moderation, is never a choice. The reason anorexia is so hard to treat is because the child has found the "perfect solution" to not getting fat and deep inside is extremely terrified of becoming obese. Unfortunately, many young people die from anorexia. Bulimia (binging and purging) has many of the same attractions as anorexia. The overeating feels nurturing and quiets the emotional pain in seeming to fill that black empty hole, and the purging creates an endorphin high, along with avoiding weight gain. Obesity is nationally recognized as a cause of severe health problems but is still not uniformly recognized as an addiction. It has been recognized for decades as the most difficult disorder-related problem to treat. It involves more denial than any other addiction, despite and because of its visual manifestation. Moderation is not a choice in an addictive family.

Another factor that I have found to be frequent, if not prevalent, with eating disorders is some form of sexual abuse in the person's history. The body form with obesity is seen as unattractive, therefore, safe from sexual approach, and also has a feeling of safety in the bulk of it. For the anorexic female, there is often long delay of physical development into womanhood, giving an almost male appearance that is less attractive to a male. Virtually all of my eating disordered clients have shared that they experienced some form of sexual abuse or incest as a child, sometimes followed by a rape experience as a young female, which has left them sexually dysfunctional.

The money-addictive process encompasses several compulsive behaviors, but all are dysfunctional and cause problems. Gambling, of course, often paired with sex addiction, is only one version of money addiction. It is a progressive compulsion of the addiction disease, like other medicators. Many families are financially ruined or live a life that vacillates back and forth from feast to famine because of mom or dad's relationship with money addiction, whether it is gambling (stock market also can be a form of gambling), overspending, or hoarding.

Religious addiction, known in the addictions treatment community as religiosity, is sometimes a major issue in a dysfunctional family. This happens when one of the major caretakers is obsessed with a particular religion in a fanatical way. The closed system is very controlling for the children, shame producing, and fear-based. Children often grow up either obsessed with the same fanatical beliefs or in complete rebellion they can become atheist or agnostic. Either way it can, and does, shut down the possibility of finding their spiritual path. Statistics have shown that there is a higher than average rate of alcoholism stemming out of these families. This points to the fact that human beings do not like to be controlled or heavily shamed, and it is the nature of humans to search out their answers.

Shopping addiction, which is referred to as being a "shopaholic," is another very prevalent form of addiction. This most often is seen in women, who are compulsive about buying more clothes and shoes. This makes sense in terms of the female image, massively promoted and sold by advertising. I have noted that even women who can afford quite a bit carry a sense of guilt about compulsive shopping. Many have closets full of clothes with the tags still on, never worn. Buying things to fill the emotional hole is rampant in our society. It fits right in with looking good and the decoration of outer self to cover up the pain of the inner self. The belief is that one more piece of clothing, or another electronic gadget, or a prettier, pricier home or car can make one okay. Many adult children have grown up in homes, where despite severe dysfunction and near poverty, they try to look good at all costs. Thus, for example, when taking the family to church, mosque, synagogue, or other outings, they make sure to be well-dressed, perhaps even when there is not enough furniture or other necessities at home. Even in the poorest of families, there is usually a shopping dysfunction. making the situation more difficult, and thus many parental conflicts ensue.

Many of you may already know a good bit about or have grown up with alcohol and drug addiction. Again, that relationship is primary and supersedes all other relationships. There is constant disappointment in family members' relationships with the addict, as they do not come first. The family becomes emotionally and psychologically infected with the addiction disease, feeling powerless over it, as they truly are. But, part of the family disease is that they learn to enable it by deluding themselves into believing the addict surely will see the problem and stop using. They also accept it as normal, long into the disease progression, especially if the non-alcoholic parent grew up in an alcoholic family. The children have to accept it, because the parents do. Much anger and pain is swallowed in the family, as a result of verbal abuse, physical abuse, sexual abuse, and shame. Generally, the addict's spouse is love/hate addicted to the addict, obsessed with the disease, and the family functions around the disease. Children have no one who puts them first. The relationship with addiction destroys the family, and the children are destined to repeat this relationship.

Two of the more recently recognized addictions are sex and love addictions. We come out of dysfunctional families with a starvation for love in many ways. This creates many dysfunctional relationships in our lives, because we usually do not have a fully identified Self. What we refer to as the primary disease of love addiction is when a person is relationship addicted. This means there is a willingness to give up Self in the hope of being loved in a relationship. It never works, because love addiction means one does not love Self. If I do not love myself — and how can I, if no one ever treated me as loveable — I cannot internalize another's love of me. Add to this, that as a love addict, I unknowingly will still choose a partner or even friends who abuse me as my family did. The dilemma about domestic abuse is that it combines the love/hate childhood wounds of the perpetrator with the love addiction of their partner, who cannot let go. The love addict lives in the same delusions of thinking that the perpetrator (usually male) will change, like the partner of an alcoholic believes the alcoholic

Anne Salter, LCSW

will change. Love addiction does not always involve violence, but it will involve giving oneself away and often will include multiple abandonments. Relationship with love addiction is not about love; it is about neediness.

Sex addiction is a relationship with one's sexuality that has, from being inappropriately sexually energized, become a way to get a fix without becoming emotionally intimate. Orgasm is often described as giving as much of a high as is experienced from heroin. Many sex addicts, but not all are what I describe in the roles we adapt as lost children. They gave up on people in their early years and tend to meet their needs alone, involving minimal connection with people and not becoming emotionally intimate. Having a relationship for the sex addict mostly will involve masturbation, pornographic materials, especially on the Internet today, prostitutes, one-night stands, or any and all of the above. Many spend a tremendous amount of hours doing one or all of these things to seek relief. The relationship with sex addiction develops out of loneliness, a need to medicate wounded feelings, and is an outcome of some kind of sexual abuse in the family of origin. Addiction to pornography and to the Internet has/have greatly increased one's isolation in sex addiction and stimulated the availability of a faster progression into the disease, such as child pornography.

There are many stories of sexual abuse that involve direct violence, such as on-going intercourse by adults with children. However, people often don't realize that the effects of less direct or physically abusive sex also can have profound effects on a child, and many develop sex addiction from this. This is often referred to as emotional sex abuse. In a previous chapter, I wrote several stories of people who I have known with sex addiction.

Finally, there is relationship with work as an addiction. Actually, this includes the issue of what I refer to as "busy-a-holism." Keeping busy, whether it is being married to one's job or always on the go with projects, or helping others (or trying to fix them) keeps one from feeling, which is the goal of addictions: not to think or feel those wounds, fears, and insecurities. So, work-aholism is seen in the lack of moderation in behavioral activities.

Many adult children have some degree of this work addiction. It is most prevalent with those who have been in the family role of hero child, as described in other chapters. This child has adapted early on to becoming a major caretaker, doer, and accomplisher. There is no end to the ways in which she/he attempts to get good enough or to please family. Even though as an adult, he/she is unaware that pleasing the family is still the force behind the drive to accomplish. It then gets transferred to adult behavior and relationships. Traditionally in our society, this constantly driven personality has been written off as just a normal A personality type, rather than as dysfunctional. The person who is thus driven often experiences extreme stress and eventual burn-out. The relationship with work and play also becomes an addictive relationship. Children experience a lot of abandonment when they have a workaholic parent.

Relationships with addiction is a major factor in an unfulfilled life. Adult children from any dysfunctional family usually have some relationship with addiction. Addictions cover up old wounds and leave us unable to be available for true intimacy, which is what everyone truly longs to have yet fears.

The only recovery programs with a proven high percentage on recovery are the 12-step programs. These provide support, fellowship, group sharing, a roadmap for getting and staying sober, and a spiritual aspect. Those who are seeking to help someone get into recovery need to remember that addiction is a mental disease, making it impossible for the addict to make a healthy choice or recover alone.

Questionnaire on Relationship with Addictions

A core issue in our development of Self and choices in Relationships

1. Was or is there addiction in your family of origin? Who? Describe how you feel it has had an effect on you.
2. Describe your family-of-origin's relationship with addictions, including grandparents.
3. Do you recognize a relationship with addiction in yourself? Describe it in depth.
4. What or who most affected you in your family of origin and ancestry with addictions? How?

RELATIONSHIP WITH MATES, SIGNIFICANT OTHERS, AND LOVERS

Who stands between us?

This is the chapter you may have been waiting for!?
I say this because most people think this is the only thing
that we have a relationship with: love interests. I hope by now it is
clear to you that we have relationships with everything in our lives,
some more important than others. Certainly the relationship with
one's spouse or love interest is very important, in fact, hopefully
the most important one. No doubt, you already have formulated
many ideas about these relationships and how much they are
affected by one's "stew-pot."

Relationship with a spouse or with another committed person requires more of us than any other relationship in our lives since childhood (if we had to adapt in our childhood). For it to be fulfilling, it requires the qualities of a healthy adult, whose physical and emotional needs were met as a child. This adult will have good self-esteem, a well-formed identity, and a healthy separation from family of origin, followed by a continued healthy connection with family of origin. He/she will not be looking unconsciously for self-fulfillment from another person. A close relationship will add to an already self-actualized person, who doesn't need to fill an emotional void created from family of origin.

Looking at the fallout from one's "family stew" and probably ancestral, as well, there are so many ways in which one's choice of and one's ability to function in a potentially intimate and permanent relationship will be affected. After family of origin, this will be the first potential possibility one can have to experience true safety, harmony, and adult fulfillment.

For those of us from dysfunctional families, the problems begin right away in the choosing. There is a saying that we have "a broken picker" when we choose relationships. Inevitably, we will choose a person who, like us, has unresolved issues with family of origin and, therefore, carries baggage. Our choice also will be someone, who in some ways, is like our parent(s) and usually with behaviors of the parent with whom we have the most unresolved issues. Amazingly, we choose someone with whom we will continue to have the same issues and conflicts. Rather than choosing someone who can nurture our wounds or help us to resolve them, we choose someone who will unwittingly salt the wounds, causing them to grow deeper.

A good example would be those who had a very critical parent inevitably will choose someone who also had a critical parent, and then they become critical of one another. Thus, the wounds get deeper and intimacy is distanced. For many who have been severely abused and their self-esteem diminished, choosing a mate will mean picking someone who, though it doesn't appear that way, will severely abuse them. This choice, of course, will be someone who has also been abused and/or witnessed abuse, often of one parent abusing the other. This is the tragedy of what we refer to as domestic abuse. Treatment for this, which usually involves the man as the perpetrator, is court-ordered classes for learning anger control. The problem with this solution is that the anger/rage, which is perpetrated onto the mate, comes from a much deeper level. The anger belongs to family of origin. Without treating these perpetrators as victims of early abuse and working to resolve their anger issues with techniques of emotionally expressive family-of-origin therapy, there is almost no like likelihood of controlling this anger. Anger is often triggered by unconscious wounds, compelling the perpetrator to act out of control.

When we talk about triggers in the process of recovery from addictions, we must recognize and be aware of what triggers us emotionally to relapse into drinking and drugging, or other means of medicating to numb emotional pain. In relationships, especially close ones, triggers are a very important part of losing ourselves to old wounds. First, we experience transference, defined again as putting certain characteristics, meanings of behaviors, and intentions for someone else onto another person. Thus, we are triggered by someone or something they say or do, because we are not seeing/hearing that person, but are reacting to someone from our family of origin. When this happens we interpret a suggestion from a mate as criticism. It is greatly intensified because of the raw wounds from being criticized as a child. As an adult, there is an angry retort or accusation, rather than a response that might correct the situation. The interchange becomes heated, often fraught with blame, and there is more hurt as a result. These altercations stockpile, as have our original wounds that never got resolved, thus destroying trust. There can be no emotional intimacy without trust. Trust is probably the greatest barrier adult children of dysfunctional families incur when attempting to form an intimate relationship. Each occurrence of hurt creates more distance from intimacy.

One can be triggered by many other things beside criticism. If there has been sexual abuse in any form in the family of origin, then there will be sexual problems in relationship, many times blocking true intimacy. A sexually abused child has been violated in the deepest way, and the memory, even sometimes only a body memory, will be easily triggered. An example of a body memory would be when a person reacts negatively to a non-violating touch from a trusted loved one, which would normally be an acceptable touch. This even could be from a touch to a non-sexual part of the body. A reaction to a smell that is normally not offensive could also be a trigger. In whatever way this person was sexually energized will determine what sexual behaviors he/she is attracted to, fulfilled or repelled by, or why he/she is unable to perform. Often this person will choose either another sexual perpetrator, someone else who has been abused in some way, or someone who has experienced sexual dysfunction in his/her family of origin. Sometimes, it can be that the mate grew up in a family where the opposite sex was not respected or was taught to expect sex without showing sensitivity.

Difficulty with the personal relationship between two people is not all that is affected by family of origin. Many more things must be worked out for the best of the couple-ship, such as where to live, the allocation of responsibilities, MONEY MANAGEMENT, how to parent (e.g., one person believes in spanking, the other does not), what kind of friends to have or which friends to share, whether to have pets, whether to travel, issues with alcohol or drug use, and agreement on hobbies and passions, etc.

Relationship sounds really challenging when you look at this list, which is still far from complete. Adult children have either grown up with dysfunctional skills or no guidelines on these issues, other than to perpetuate what their parents did or to react by doing just the opposite. Opposite or extreme behaviors will have the same negative results. Adult children compulsively react as a result of their wounds, rather than respond, which would be healthy behavior.

Delores, who is married to Jim, wants to use some of their money to travel. Jim is not interested in traveling and views this as a waste of money, which they may need for more important things. They argue. She has different needs than he does. She has a potentially terminal disease, and wants to do all she can while she is still functional. He fears there will not be enough money to take care of them when she progresses in her illness, requiring more medical care. She came from a family where she never had much of anything, but her mother modeled spending on self. He came from a family where he also had very little and is afraid of ending up without, thus wanting to live frugally. They are trapped in their extreme positions, reacting to childhood experiences and a lack of healthy parenting.

Joe grew up in a small apartment in a city. Sonia grew up in a home in the suburbs, where there was a large lawn with plenty of space. Her parents argued about many things concerning the home, such as Dad complaining about the never-ending lawn work, and Mom complaining about the cleaning and repairs needed for such a large home. Sonia, who felt isolated from the arts and culture that would be more accessible in the city, made a decision as a child that she wanted to live and to raise her family in a nice apartment in the city. Joe, on the other hand, wanted the nice big home in the suburbs, which his parents had dreamed of having, one without the lack of space in an apartment and away from the noise of the city. We do not know what their choices might have been, had there not been arguments and dysfunction about the home in their families of origin. Neither Joe nor Sonia was aware of how much they were influenced by their history. This kind of conflict often is impossible to resolve when there is no room for compromise, such as choosing a reasonably large or middle-sized home near the city. Adult children see most things in black and white with no gray areas. Healthy adults are able to be open to other options, which can lead to healthy compromise.

As a child, Bobby was made to sleep outside in the smelly, cold, flea-infested doghouse, as punishment for some behavior for which he was deemed bad. He grew up hating dogs. His wife, Betty, grew up with many dogs, which were all dear to her. She had every intention to always own a dog. When they had children, who also wanted a dog, Bobby was outnumbered, and he was angry. He rented an apartment for them, and they were told no pets were allowed when they moved in. Now, the entire family was unhappy. This created a large barrier in their relationship and made him look like the bad guy.

Tim grew up in a traditional family, where his parents and their friends rigidly were set in certain roles. The husband was the breadwinner, who came home in the evening expecting and receiving his slippers by the television set and his dinner served at precisely six o'clock. His mother was responsible for cleaning the house, taking care of the children, and taking care of his needs in a rather subservient way. Though times have changed considerably, there are still mates Tim could have chosen who would be willing to play the role his mother played. However, Tim, who unconsciously did not respect his mother, wanted a more independent woman, so he married Cathy. Cathy also grew up with a subservient mother and decided as a child, that she "would not play this role with any mate!" Though Tim thought he wanted an independent woman, he was quite shocked when Cathy, who also worked outside of the home, expected him to share household duties and child care. Tim hadn't anticipated these consequences of having an independent wife, so they were stuck.

The two most major negative outside influences on a couple-ship are alcohol/drug abuse and any other addiction, and their adult relationship with parents and in-laws. All are potential invasions, which can violate the couple-ship.

Addiction(s) mean there can be no real intimacy, because the addicted person is married to the substance, such as alcohol or to the compulsive behavior, such as gambling. Alcoholism and drug addiction, which are enabled inadvertently in families, is a mental disease, which grows more and more hurtful to everyone in the family. As I have said before, if one grows up in an addictive family he/she will almost always become an addict or partner with one or both. When there is addiction in couple-ship, I often say, "It is like having a very negative parent or in-law living with you."

The addiction affects every relationship and every decision. Children with alcoholic parent(s) grow up wounded in many areas and are prone to pass this disease along, just as it often has been passed on from previous generations. Couples cannot learn new, less hurtful communication skills, if there is an addict in the couple-ship. This is because when using, the addict automatically falls back into the old, hurtful communication and behavior. Also, an addict cannot quit using without help. A dry addict is one who has not surrendered to being an addict, is white-knuckling it, and without any help or support is constantly vulnerable to relapse. Without recovery work, the addict will still retain a lot of anger and behaviors, which were thought only to be there when using.

Infidelity is more likely to happen where there is addiction, especially if one or both of the partners carry baggage of sexual abuse or incest. Again, these sexual boundary violations create the inability to keep sexual boundaries in their adult life. Adding an addiction to alcohol or drugs, or of money power, often stimulate behaviors that cross boundaries, in the rush for a fix. For example, when one has been violated sexually by a parent or other caretaker, then the impulse to cross these boundaries and to be unfaithful to a partner are intensified by a drug like alcohol, which puts rational judgment to sleep.

The invasion of parents/in-laws in a couple-ship usually happens when there has been no healthy separation of the child from the parental relationship. Therefore, the parent does not respect the boundaries of the couple-ship or the right of their adult child to have their own life or to make their own decisions. As a result, there are invasions of privacy by parents, expecting decisions to be made with their input, believing that their grown child is still supposed to hold first allegiance to them. If there has been parent-child role reversal, then the parent expects to be taken care of by the couple. Many of these situations occur where there is large family-of-origin enmeshment (see Chapter 3: Family of Origin), or enmeshment of a particular parent with a married son or daughter. This is even more difficult for each partner with their in-laws, as this partner has no history or heart connection with these parents, other than being married to their offspring.

One such family that I knew required that their daughter, Patsy, do whatever her mother wanted, no matter how this invaded Patsy's life or her relationship with her own family. Patsy's father did not protest. Patsy was terrified of abandonment by her mother, as she had experienced how her mother abandoned others who displeased her and had abandoned Patsy as a child in many ways. The mother used manipulative, victim/martyr communication to enhance her control. Patsy's husband, Art, who came from a family where his mother had abandoned him as a young boy by leaving the family, had unresolved anger regarding his mother. Like Patsy's mother, she, too, was very self-centered, reflecting this by justifying her abandonment of Art. Patsy and Art had severe, fear-of-abandonment issues and were trapped in their inability to separate from these emotionally controlling mothers. These mothers often interrupted Art and Patsy's ability to focus on their relationship and on their children.

Paula and Clem wanted to take vacations. However, Clem's family insisted and expected that they visit them whenever they had vacation time. Paula's family did not insist on this and lived closer, so Clem became the one who had to defend his need to do as his parents wished. They always went to see his parents, preventing extended vacations elsewhere. He would feel guilty to even tell them he wanted to go elsewhere, even though it would be a perfectly reasonable desire, and not to be taken personally, as a rejection of his parents. So, he never did. He was afraid of their disapproval, which obviously was very effective in getting their way.

If you have ever wondered why you have difficulty in love relationships and/or seem to end up with the same kind of relationship you had as a child, perhaps now, you can see why this is true. It's very unfortunate and sad that the two most important decisions we make in life — choosing a mate and the parenting of children — are so fraught with pain. If only personal counselling was encouraged or even possibly required before committing to a relationship, then perhaps one could better understand one's Self first and, consequently, be more aware when choosing a mate.

QUESTIONNAIRE FOR RELATIONSHIP WITH MATES, SIGNIFICANT OTHERS, AND LOVERS

1. Was there infidelity in your parents' marriage? Did you know about it as a child?
2. If you have children, how have your partner relationship(s) reflected in parenting?
3. Have you had in-laws? If so, how has that affected your partner relationship and your parenting?
4. What other conflicts in couple-ship can you see were fallout from family or origin?
5. Did your parents argue a lot? Do you?

Chapter Eighteen

RELATIONSHIP WITH WORK, CAREER, AUTHORITY AND CO-WORKERS

Achievement, or Repeated Failure?

After all that has been loaded into one's self computer, it can be easy to see how relationships with our jobs/careers, bosses, and co-workers can be effected if we grew up in a dysfunctional family. I attended a workshop that showed how an office, agency, or an institution becomes like a family. Sadly, there are many work environments that are dysfunctional, and in the office, like in the family, the health or un-healthiness of a business flows from the head down. The bosses are the parents, and the workers are the siblings. In an office, the workers inevitably will fall into the roles that they adapted in their family of origin. There will be a scapegoat, a hero, a lost child, and a mascot. In large offices, there will be more than one person in each role.

The hero will be the busiest worker, always trying to impress the boss, striving to be the No.1 favorite of the boss, doing extra work, and often becoming a workaholic. Those in the lost child role also will be good workers, keep more to themselves and strive to get into a more individual position of power, such as a supervisory position, where they can isolate more and be in charge/control. The mascots often will be the office clowns or try to keep things cheerful, prevent or interrupt arguments, often behave immaturely, and even try to compete with other employees, although they have fewer skills. The scapegoats will have the most trouble, for they inevitably will have issues with authority, having been picked on/blamed at home, ending up with a chip on the shoulder. They will interpret most instructions from the boss as criticism whether constructive or not and will find fault with the boss, ending up leaving or getting fired. The scapegoat will have had an adversarial relationship with one parent or both, will have a huge need to be right, and will think of and possibly refer to the boss disrespectfully, such as "an idiot who doesn't know anything." These transference issues with the boss (authority figure) will lead to him/her leaving the job with no awareness of their part in creating the problems and may spend many years going from job to job. The scapegoat sees the world and people as potential enemies, especially those in authority positions, as they relate back to how authority was handled negatively at home.

These job/career-related transference symptoms are some of the worst fallout from these dysfunctional roles, which are carried into adulthood. All of these roles put the adult child survivor in a fear-based state of being, worrying about getting approval, trying to move up in a job, or worrying about work siblings who may be favored. It is a mental/emotional transference from childhood, having had a lack of effective nurture and boundary-based parenting. This, in itself, is a way of carrying family-of- origin trauma into adult life and situations.

From the age of five, James grew up in a one-parent home with his mother and four children. Andrea, the oldest, took on the hero role. Second born were twins: James and John. James became a mascot/scapegoat, who struggled with Andrea, wanting her hero role. John became a lost child, who eventually dropped out on drugs. Sam, born last, became another lost child. James grew up with low self-esteem, much related to his father's leaving and the fact that his father didn't connect with the children. James was full of anger and hurt toward his physician father for leaving them without much financial support. His father would deny him special things he asked for, though he could well afford them. His mother, who worked full time, struggled to pay bills, having little help from his father, and also was absent a lot dating, trying to fill her needs.

James, like many mascots, disguised his low self-esteem with grandiosity. He made it through his education despite heavy drug use, received a professional degree, and started his own business. He became a workaholic, who drove his employees too hard and took on far too many projects. When asked how much money and success would be enough, he wasn't able to answer within any set boundaries. He desperately wanted his father's approval and to prove that he was the most successful child in his family. His work-aholism and relentless schedule caused him to neglect his marriage, to have frequent blow-ups with his wife and children, and to always to be in a rush.

Mary was the scapegoat in her family, one of four children, and the only girl. Her father was chauvinistic, disconnected (himself a lost child), and teased her along with her three brothers and saying inappropriate things about women. Her mother was emotionally unavailable, a hero/scapegoat herself, and still trying to achieve something that would impress her own mother. Mary became very angry. She acted out until these dysfunctional parents could not control her and put her in a long-term treatment facility for teenagers. As the scapegoat to all of them, Mary ended up with deep authority issues, a need to be right, to be important, and to be respected. Sadly, though, the relationship skills she had developed in this adversarial, out-of-control family, were negative. Mary was smart but had very little self-esteem. She carried a lot of chaotic emotional baggage, had trouble focusing on building a career, or getting through school. She, too, had a chip on her shoulder, always ended up in altercations with her bosses, and then had to leave or to be let go from her job. She became more blaming and grandiose each time. Her self-esteem slipped further. She had learned to be the scapegoat, so it came naturally to her to become grandiose and to challenge her superiors. Mary was not aware of how she set this up, over and over, each time ending up financially broke and getting rescued either by her parents, a boyfriend, or another friend. She deluded herself by thinking she was independent and had always taken care of herself. Fortunately, in her early 40s, she found a resource who took her through her family-of-origin experiences at an emotional level, and she has been able to free herself from some of her family baggage. Everything in her life has changed, especially her relationships. Now, she is able to find out who she really is, rather than the adapted role in her family, and to realize her dreams and achievements.

As a lost child, Donna knew she wanted to get out of her chaotic, out-of-control, frightening, alcoholic, abusive home as soon as possible. At age sixteen, she managed to get a scholarship to college and left home with only the clothes on her back. She worked her way through college, isolating there, too. When she got out of school, she found work in an insurance company, where she was able to become a favorite of the boss by working many extra hours and being reliable. She was then given a supervisory position, which helped her to isolate. After a few years, she established her own business and did not have to be close to anyone as the boss. She was never a peer, which is when one really can connect, but instead remained separate and in control of people.

All children want to be No. 1, in the favored spot with their parents. These adaptive roles are the way in which they strive for the attention or for a special place. For most of us, whatever role or roles we took on, we see the hero role as the place to be in a dysfunctional family. Remember, these roles are not who we are but are adapted to get our parents' attention/ approval. Even the most rebellious of us do this. A scapegoat child often adapts a hero role later in life. A mascot usually tries to become the hero. The lost child adapts the hero role by achieving career and/or financial success as an adult. The roadblocks for us are the defenses we have formed, our distorted views of people, especially those in authoritative roles and our distorted views of which behaviors are productive. The hero role is really one of the hardest, because the expectations this child forms for Self are unreachable, like those of James, who could not place a limit on how much he needed to achieve. (Also, remember a story I told in Chapter 2: Relationship with Family of Origin, about the boy who strove to become his dead hero brother.) Hero children often burn out. This is because the hero child, as an adult, still strives for parental approval, even though childhood is over, and is not striving to please and actualize Self.

In our efforts to realize our potential, we are unaware that we are still imprisoned in our family of origin and continue to repeat those childhood experiences in the form of transferences in the workplace.

QUESTIONNAIRE ON WORK RELATIONSHIPS

1. Can you recognize a role that you have played in your work/career?
2. Do you get stuck in authority issues, as a pattern, with job criticism?
3. Write a short history of your jobs/careers and look for patterns.
4. Do you get along well with most fellow employees?
5. If you are a boss, do you drive your employees hard? Are you critical?
6. Do you find fault a lot with others in work situations?
7. Can you delegate?
8. Are you a workaholic? Busy-a-holic? Constantly doing something?
9. Are you overly competitive?
10. Do you have specific goals and plans? Do you stick to them?
11. Do you find that you seem to still be trying to prove yourself, even though you already have?

CHAPTER NINETEEN

YOUR ADULT RELATIONSHIPS WITH FAMILY AND HOME

Have you really left your family of origin?

RELATIONSHIP WITH HOME

Your relationship with your home, whether it is an apartment or house, rented or owned, will reflect your feelings about home, which is also a reaction from your childhood. If you grew up in a comfortable, safe home(s), you will be inclined to create the same kind of home. If your home was filled with chaos, there are memories of, a drunken dad or mom in a recliner with cigarette butts spilling over the ashtray, a lot of clutter and furnishings not well kept, you most likely will want a very ordered and clean home. Or, some might just repeat the original home environment. If you avoided being home because of negative happenings, feeling unwanted, or other negative reasons, then you will find it difficult to make a close connection to your home as an adult, wanting to be somewhere else. If you were neglected as a child and not taken care of, you may find it impossible to make a good home for yourself. Whatever your experiences with home, you can trace your creating of a home, or not, and your feelings about it to your family-of-origin experience. If your family moved a lot, chances are you were unable to feel settled and connected to any home, knowing it surely would be lost when there was another move. There was no sense of belonging anywhere.

My history with home was living in a nice large house in a safe friendly neighborhood from the age of ten, until I left for college at eighteen. However, this home also was where much of my trauma was experienced. This was where my mother obsessively would clean the house, so that you would be safe to eat off the garage floor, and of course all other floors! This made my home very uncomfortable, as my mother was afraid of a mess and wanted everything perfectly in place and clean. I was not encouraged to bring friends home. She was afraid of what the neighbors might think, so she had to have everything (outside of Self) looking good. My mother was clearly unhappy and so critical, so I preferred to be out of the house as much as possible. She always would have to call my friends' houses to get me to come home. As a teenager, she would yell at me and threaten me about cleaning my room. Then, she would clean it while I was out. At night, I was afraid to go to sleep, afraid of my father sometimes roaming around drunk, and would sometimes sneak out and go up the street to my friend's house to stay over, sneaking home early the next morning.

When I went away to college and later started a career, I kept my apartment very messy and piled my clothes in a closet, until I sent them to the cleaners. I always have hated housework, always paid someone to do it, and for many years I was on the go and seldom home. It was quite a number of years before I created a home that I connected to emotionally and one where I wanted to be at home.

One of my clients has been unable to make a home for himself. He was very abused and abandoned, and he left on his own as a child, so he has no sense of belonging anywhere. Added to this, the apartments where he lived in the city were unkempt by his parents, there was constant fighting and name calling, and the streets around were full of unsafe men, who would use little boys. He spent much of his childhood riding the subway train, going to museums and other places that kept him away from where he lived. No one cared that he was missing or how much danger he was in, though he was only seven or eight years old. He learned that he was not worth being taken care of or of making a home for him-self. He treats himself the same way that his family did.

Another person I know grew up in another country, and his father was in the military. They moved frequently, their household furnishings belonged to the Army, and they often could not take many of their possessions. He left home at fifteen and lived in a rented room, furnished only with a bed and books. He was able to escape in his head by reading books. When I first met him, he lived sparsely with few possessions. This, of course, was a childhood lesson learned: "Don't get attached to things, for you will lose them." He naturally married a woman who liked to have things and this caused conflicts. In general, he was very selfish with himself, from being treated as if he deserved nothing as a child. In addition to this, his father was a severe alcoholic, and it was chaotic and abusive wherever they lived.

Willa grew up extremely deprived emotionally, physically, and spiritually. The experience of so much poverty was reflected in her choices of new, clean, and modern homes, and in her collecting and hoarding of things. This hoarding and saving the best of two items (only using the most tattered or old for herself), and shopping for bargains reflected her fears about money and poverty. As Willa aged, she accumulated more and more things, most never being used, and her home became cluttered. Widowed from the husband who had provided well for her, she could not bring herself to pay for better things. When she died, this woman, who had kept a clean, neat, uncluttered home as a young wife and mother, left huge plastic bags full of items she had collected, for which she had no use. Her home reflected her reaction to the poverty of her childhood, which had never been resolved.

I invite you to look at your home and your feelings about it. Does it reflect your fears and family emotional baggage?

ADULT RELATIONSHIPS WITH PARENTS

If we come from a dysfunctional family, then we leave home with emotional baggage and unfinished business. As I have said before, this is reflected in our people relationships through transference reactions.

If we are emotionally healthy when we go off to college or move out of our parents home, we would expect to be independent, make decisions, soon pay our own bills, and begin our own lives. However, with emotional baggage, this rarely happens in functional healthy ways.

One of the ways that adult children of dysfunctional families hang on to family of origin is by expecting or requiring their parents to continue supporting them financially. In many dysfunctional families, money and things are given instead of love. The recipient of these love substitutes continues to need the emotional love and approval. But, having experienced that money means love, they will continue to expect this financial support from the parents. Parents often resent this but out of guilt continue to provide this kind of support, which further handicaps the adult child, stunting their self-esteem and growth even more.

In my work in the addictions field, I have worked with many families, whose son or daughter, now in their thirties, has never managed to finish school (paid for by parents) and/or settle into a job that supports them. The parents have continued to bail this son or daughter out of problems with drugs from being irresponsible, and they continue to support them financially, often more than necessary. Thus, the adult child believes in Self even less and expects to be supported. It is the most important task, as a therapist, to teach the parents to let go, so that the child can grow up! These children have been referred to over the years as spoiled, as if that were a character flaw in the child. What spoiled really means is that they have been fed with money and things, instead of love and boundaries. This, perpetrated by the parents, spoils them. They are really just deprived emotionally and reacting to what they have been taught.

Parents, who are fear-based, over-controlling, and/or over-protective, have trouble letting their children fail, take their bumps and bruises, or take necessary risks, for them to grow up. These adult children basically will be stuck as an emotional teenager, as are most addicts before recovery work, and will internally not feel capable of making decisions and being responsible.

Finally, the saddest fallout for adult children is when they marry or are in a partnership and still depend on parents, allowing them and their opinions and ideas to supercede their partner's. They do not have appropriate boundaries established between the couple and the parents.

You can now see why we all need to decathect (separate our childhood connection from our parents) and form an adult-to-adult relationship with our parents when we grow up. We need to leave home emotionally.

RELATIONSHIP WITH IN-LAWS

Those of us from dysfunctional homes often are very surprised by the difficult relationship that can develop with in-laws. Very often the in-laws, unless they clearly don't like their son or daughter's chosen mate, will seem to be very loving and excited to bring the mate into the family. We can get tricked in many ways. For example, after the honeymoon is over, the in-laws may become invasive, visiting without calling first, feeling that the couple's home is theirs, giving unsolicited advice, or always taking their adult child's side if there is disagreement in the coupleship. Another surprise can be that you are close, or so you thought, to your mother-in-law, but you become the enemy when you and your husband separate, instead of receiving efforts to help resolve the problems. Or, there can be over-involvement with your struggles when you do not want their input. Remember, it doesn't matter whose parents they are, they will all overstep their boundaries if they are dysfunctional, because they don't have healthy ones.

Sometimes, you have had a parent with whom you didn't get along or felt rejected by, and you get into the fantasy that the parent-in-law is just the father/mother you always wanted. You may get lucky occasionally, but remember if you come from a dysfunctional family, you can be sure that your chosen mate has also, even though it might not seem apparent until further into the relationship. We tend to choose people relative to us in how healthy or dysfunctional we are.

If your family of origin and/or your mate's families are enmeshed (see Chapter 3: Themes from our Family of Origin), then this lack of de-cathexis will be a major block in your coupleship.

Finally, in-laws may have very different ideas about how children should be raised, such as in religion, parenting styles, discipline, etc. You need to be clear with your partner early on and agree on what your family will look like in terms of these issues, as well as setting clear boundaries with parents and in-laws.

Relationship with Children

First, let me say, that however you were parented will very much dominate your choices in parenting. You may continue much like your parents or resolve to do the opposite. Either of these extremes will be dysfunctional, but our childhood experiences have programmed us to do what was done to us, or, in a child's mind, to do the opposite.

If you grew up with a very controlling parent, you probably will be over-controlling also, and because your style will be different, you will be very surprised when your children tell you that you are very controlling. If you grew up with parents who abandoned you or you did not feel safe, you may not know how to protect your child or will become very over-protective. Polarities create the same outcomes. Both an abandoned child and an over-protected child will have low self-esteem and lack confidence.

You will find yourself shocked that you are critical or hit your child, becuase you hated these behaviors done to you as a child. As I have said, our mental memory computers are loaded with experience data, and we automatically react from these old, stored experiences when in a similar situation, such as in parenting a child.

Most people, if they want children, want to be a good parent, but haven't a clue about how to accomplish this. I remember when I stopped doing some negative things to my children, I felt like I was in a vacuum when a situation occurred, where I only knew one reaction. I would call my friend, a healthy parent, and ask her what to do. I was able to slowly change my dysfunctional parenting skills, but not as soon as I would have liked.

One of the saddest things that some of us experience is having abusive parents, perhaps one parent who seemed to hate you, and then having a chronologically grownup child, who treats you the same way. It is like double abuse and will take a lot of professional help to stop perpetuating this type of familial dysfunction.

Someone I knew many years ago, named Joan, came to my home for a celebration and brought her three-year-old child. At one point, I glanced out on my back patio where our pool was, and the little child was wandering alone around the pool. When I gently confronted Joan about the danger and that the child needed to be watched, she responded that the child would have to learn her own lessons, and she wasn't going to try to control everything the child did. I was horrified! Today, I realize that Joan had grown up with a very over-controlling mother and decided to stay out of her daughter's way, to the extent of not even protecting her.

Questionnaire on Your Adult Relationships with Family and Home

1. What is your relationship with your home since you moved out from your childhood home? How is it the same or different? Do you see ways in which it has been influenced by your childhood home(s)?
2. Describe your relationship as an adult with your parents and relatives. Does it reflect that there is unresolved emotional baggage? Does it interfere with your adult life and with your family?
3. If you have in-laws, how is this relationship? Does it create conflicts with your partner?
4. Describe your relationship with your children. Does it look in any or many ways similar to your relationships with your parents? Are you compulsively repeating behaviors that you hated and feeling guilty and powerless?

Chapter Twenty

RELATIONSHIP WITH THE WORLD AT LARGE AND POLITICS

How Does This Relate to Self-History and Values?

JOHN LENNON WROTE AND SANG: "IMAGINE
ALL THE PEOPLE LIVING IN PEACE ..."

RELATIONSHIP WITH THE WORLD AT LARGE

In many ways, I am astounded that as a world we are still at war. When I look at history, I see very clearly how we have been, and continue to be, stuck with religious differences, and we continue to go to war thinking it will be resolved. But it never ends. Though our values in the United States are much more humane than in many other countries, we still go to war to try to change other countries to our way of viewing what is *right*. We then face them with the same theme we are bringing, whether they are ignorant of what we are proposing or whether they have abusive, mentally ill leaders who destroy them. The theme is the same, and it has never solved things over centuries of warring people—and clearly not when there are religious differences. Because we have never learned to connect with our "enemies," we don't use diplomacy effectively, and we end up going to war. Our ancestors emigrated here from all over the world to have something better. Yet they brought with them little ability to resolve relationships without ongoing conflicts, whether in the home or in broader relationships. My studies of the history in Europe, Asia, and the Americas have shown this ongoing pattern. There is a history of greed involved too; it's not about just changing people's ideas and way of life but also about taking their land and ruling over them. I feel so very discouraged and fearful today when I hear some of our politicians strongly implying that *another war* may be the answer. In twelve-step programs, we have a saying that doing the same thing over and over while expecting a different outcome is the definition of *insanity*! The idea of fighting another war as the *solution* comes from a place of fear, and we often react to fear with aggression.

Much of this may already seem obvious to you, but perhaps you haven't thought about how your childhood, schooling, and other experiences have shaped your political beliefs, your prejudices, your attitudes toward world events and toward people of different color or differing religious beliefs, and your preferences in a wide variety of issues. Do you also have a belief about war as a solution?

If your family of origin, and perhaps your ancestral "stew pot," includes behaviors and beliefs that are very rigid, controlling, and distrustful of ideas outside theirs, do not be surprised if your own attitudes, world views, and behaviors reflect this. Escaping our roots or redefining our belief systems is a very difficult task. Most of us just leave our childhood as chronological (not necessarily emotionally mature) adults and proceed to surround ourselves with others who think, believe, and behave much like our family

Anne Salter, LCSW

of origin. Some, like myself, may turn the opposite way, wishing for a different identity—but most do not.

I left my familial and ancestral closed system of beliefs that included a rigid political position, prejudices of color, and fundamentalist religion (a small southern town) and migrated to an open melting pot of ideas and beliefs, full of people of many colors, creeds, etc. I moved to New York City at age nineteen. I attended a college that offered courses on a wide array of teachings, including subjects on politics, religion, history, etc. I am not sure why I was able to make such a maverick step, from a closed to an open system, but I am so grateful today.

Closed systems of belief are much like brainwashing, as the beliefs and attitudes we carry from a closed system go very deep and are usually loaded with fear and shame. I believe the hardest belief system to change is that of fundamentalist religion, as it includes so much shaming and fear, often deeply rooted in one's "inner child." When it is flooded into a small child's brain, it becomes a deep emotional belief, which includes fear of shame and death if the beliefs and behaviors that it requires are abandoned. It is at once exclusive of other people of other paths and of permission to learn, so it naturally creates a very limited and distorted view of the world. Another example is when a political party holds its members hostage to go along with whatever the leaders decide is the only position to take on an issue, and the consequence of doing otherwise would be shunning and/or expulsion from that party. Shunning, by the way, is a practice of some of the fundamentalist religions. When this happens in politics, it becomes about the party and its internal members and *not about the people they represent.*

Within these rigid religious and political groups there is usually a lot of *hidden* prejudice, because to openly expose it would certainly put them in danger of being clearly seen in their rigid, noninclusive beliefs. When one is part of a rigid, closed system, it naturally requires one to be hypocritical and to contradict oneself, because the beliefs are black-and-white thinking, meaning that one thinks in absolutes. There are no grays. This is a major dynamic in closed systems. For example, something is either all good or all bad. These systems are loaded with what have been labeled "adult children" of dysfunctional families, who continue to be dysfunctional in many of their relationships.

What then happens in these belief systems regarding the world? Quite naturally, they are motivated to change/get rid of differing beliefs. Thus, they are usually in favor of war (versus diplomacy) as a solution to problems with other countries, excluding "nonbelievers" from their midst, enthusiastically trying to convert others to their beliefs, and using shunning and shaming as efforts to hold on to members.

I grew up as a Christian, learning the stories about Jesus and the Old Testament. Today I do not have a religious affiliation, but I believe that what Jesus strove for (and all the prophets of the Jewish and Muslim and Hindu religions, which were primary religions at that time in history, some two thousand years ago) was to connect people, to teach them to be patient and accepting, and to "love thy neighbor as thyself." He told us, "Inasmuch as ye have done it to one of the least of these my brethren, ye have done it unto me" (Matthew 25:40). What has happened to these messages, as the main message Jesus and others imparted? I do not see or experience these beliefs or behaviors today in much of our world's "religious" community. What I see is people fighting to overtake others with their religious beliefs and trying to bring them into government laws and policies

QUESTIONNAIRE ON RELATIONSHIP WITH THE WORLD

1. How did your family of origin relate to/interact with people who had different ideas from theirs on politics? On religion? Did they express prejudice sometimes, frequently, or not at all?
2. Did your family interact with those of different races, ethnic groups, etc., or only with people more similar to them?
3. Did your family encourage you to explore other beliefs, and/or did they promote education?
4. Did your parents have higher education?
5. How do you interact in relationship to the above four questions?
6. Did your family travel with you to experience other cultures or take advantage of opportunities to meet and interact with them on a local level?
7. What are your beliefs about the world at large? The problems in the Middle East?
8. Do you believe that war is a real solution to problems in/with other countries? If so, why?

Relationship with Government and Politics

As with all chapters in this book, my motive is to help people learn how their own history chooses their relationships and how each of us is connected to everyone and everything. It affects the entire world. This can be equally true in our relationship with government and politics as it is with other relationships, and it is no less valid in our choices of leaders and the values that they project. I am also motivated by a lot of fear about people voting without full awareness and knowledge of facts about the candidates. We need to look at their histories and behaviors and their party positions. These will speak best to what they are about, what their *values* are, and what they *stand for.* Is all of this congruent with what they are *saying*? I am aware that fear, ignorance (lack of knowledge), unhealthy loyalty, transference of unresolved anger, and prejudice are all motivating factors in many people's choices, including those people running for office. The four things that can most negatively affect election outcomes are ignorance, a sense of loyalty not deserved, previous religious and racial indoctrination, and *hearing only what one wants to hear, in spite of the facts.*

Government and politics are a major focus today in the minds of most people. Not only is our government trying to function in a very chaotic time, but most of the major countries around the world are in terrible upheaval. Please note that in the most violent uprisings it is about *relationship with the government.* These are governments that do not care about their people. They are controlled by money-greedy and power-hungry narcissists (or worse). This is about *mental health.*

Good mental health means we can *choose* our relationships and/ or beliefs, not just adopt them from others. It means we choose our relationships based on whether what we see and hear is congruent and by what *themes* we see in a person and their history. It means we do not choose to ignore certain facts, behaviors, incongruities, and ideas that don't fit with what we want to be true. Recently one politician stated: "We will not run a campaign based on *fact checkers.*" Is this one of the things some people choose not to hear? Do we not want our choices supported by facts?

I want to discuss some of the ways you can look at your relationship history to see how it has shaped your beliefs in this area. You may want to review the chapters on your relationships with your main mentors, and particularly those on family, teachers, religion, money, work/career, addiction, anger, and prejudice. These have profound influence on how we vote and for whom. Then look at the history (as much as you can find) on those whom you would choose as leaders. Be sure you watch their behaviors and words. Do they match? *Are they consistent?* Are the behaviors and ideas congruent, or are they contradictory to what has been presented at other times? Do their views and words seem to be constant, or do they seem to change to adjust to other people's influence? Do they have a stand on ideas that stays firm? Do they do a lot of "spinning" (making a new version or statement about the words of others that gives a different, often not true, meaning)? Do they project a lot of anger and character assassination about their opponents in their bids for office? Do they justify all this with statements in which they say, "It's just politics!"? Is this somehow said to make it less hurtful? Then, does it mean it is not true? All of this relates to whether they have *a fully defined Self,* which is certainly something we need in a leader! When I was a child we used to say that a person was *two-faced* when he or she presented one version of a subject to some people and then an opposite version to others or at other times. Isn't that just what many politicians do when they bash someone's character in one situation and then later say they are *a good friend* in another situation? "It's just politics!" No, this has no honor, and one or the other position is a lie. Is it okay to be abusive and untruthful about a friend?

Today, in the war of politics, we have some very graphic examples of lying, spinning the facts, greed, and addiction to money and power. One needs to do research, know what the *facts* are. One cannot just accept hearsay, especially from known unreliable, extremist, verbally abusive sources of information. It is also important to follow the news persistently and be aware of sources who do not do a fact check.

RELATIONSHIP WITH DENIAL, FEAR, AND ANGER

Denial is about fear. The more dysfunction in a child's home, the more denial will play a part in his or her adult life. Choices in lifestyle, partners, friends, careers, religious affiliations, and political choices will be dictated by this major defense mechanism. Closed family and religious systems create fear—fear of new ideas and of gaining broader knowledge. They create the inability to grow and to change. As I have written in the chapter on denial, we have the *ability to form our own truth* by using the defense mechanism of denial. Thus, we can eliminate facts and spin them into another viewpoint, or we can make them match what we *want the truth to be.*

Many of us have grown up with parents or other mentors who projected constant fear and always looked at the negative possibilities. This is a defense mechanism a child often adopts in order not to be surprised by frightening or negative events that *might* happen. As a grown-up, he or she will then grab on to any event or information that supports the negative view. It is a distorted way to try to feel safe. A fear of possible negative happenings relating to religion is another powerful tool to trap a person into limited choices. Too many good people are trapped in this defense mechanism, which makes risk and change out of range for them.

I want to reiterate how much *spiritual disconnect* happens when one is in denial. In the twelve-step programs, we learn that spiritual bankruptcy is a core focus related to healing addictions. In any other aspect of life, wherein our behaviors and lack of good moral choices leaves us on a path of destruction—be it of our health, our lack of financial management in our family, or our disconnect from some of our fellow Americans—we are in spiritual disconnect. This is often associated with some form of mental illness, like addiction, that leaves us out of touch with reality.

This is why when people claim that they are religious it does not always mean they are spiritually connected. Denial always involves not being connected to reality. Not connected. We can, if we are willing to look, see this in a number of our leaders. Spirituality means sharing and being willing to see the truth, whether it is what you want to be true or not. Those who undergo deep, life-changing therapy experience how difficult and painful it is at times to face truths about themselves and then to change. Adult children from dysfunctional families really hate change, and we can see the symptoms of this in a number of our politicians.

As I watch politicians and political leaders, I see so much deception. What does it mean when one is willing to lie in order to win? In order to lie, or deny the truth, you must rationalize, project blame, and minimize the facts—if you have any integrity and values you need to get around. Rationalizing is the number-one way to try to make something syntonic (fitting with one's own ego and values), since it is a manipulation of the truth to make it as close to being rational as possible and still *seem* like the truth. Today some of this is popularly called spinning. Unfortunately, not all of it is spinning. There is also outright lying.

Many of those who listen to politicians do not check the facts, so it's easy to believe in these spun truths and ever-changing positions. In addition, when lying and spinning are a major theme, those who believe them have usually grown up in dysfunctional families where this crazy-making dynamic was a normal part of family relationships—as have the politicians who are doing the lying and spinning. I grew up in one of these families; they were not bad people, just wounded people.

In this country, where we need more healing of dysfunctional relationships, we must become more aware of *Self*. This kind of mental illness (sometimes part of many psychiatric labels) can lead us to war after war, as we focus on *things* instead of each other as connected humanly and spiritually. Dysfunctional families sometimes have an outcome of greed when they try to fill the hole where they are wounded from not feeling loved. I am not a doomsayer, but Rome went down from greed and lack of spiritual connection with others. I am very much an optimist, but as I study the patterns and themes in history, the history of Rome and some parallels I see do frighten me.

PATIENCE AND ADDICTION

One of the major issues with addiction is that it is a drive for a quick fix. Americans have been called by many "an addictive society." Certainly, as a nation, we have a history that has very much enabled this. We are, I believe, a society of many people who are emotionally stuck in adolescence, teenagers still needing to grow up. A great example is the adolescent behavior of our Congress. They behave like a gang, like an immature boys' club, as they all band together and accept whatever their leaders tell them to do.

We, of course, are a very new country—a country of adult children with histories of dysfunction. In this sense, it is not a surprise that we are addictive. We have achieved so much and acquired more than most of us can handle. We have not experienced a lot of the tragedies and trials, such as untreatable plagues (AIDS is an exception), constant wars on our continent, or neighboring countries that threaten us, as have our European ancestors. We have not had to grow through those experiences. However, like many other countries, we have yet to learn from history that war does not solve anything and that change takes time.

We need to do this rebuilding of our country together. Some believe we are all *capable* of doing it individually. This is not true. We are *not* created equally in this way. Many of us need some community support, often just temporarily. This is because we have different levels of abilities, both mental and physical. This depends on our history from birth, what we came into the world with individually, our experiences, and many other factors—definitely including level of mental health. Can we learn, as individuals and as a nation, to connect to others different from us, let go of some of our European history of warring and greed, and try to really be "one nation under God" (in whatever way you choose to believe and practice, as long as it harms no one)? I believe that we can strive for this, with each individual working toward a fully defined Self and becoming connected in relationship with others who may be very different.

If we can just change our world, as each of us becomes more aware of who we are and what we project: "Imagine all the people living life in peace …" (John Lennon).

Relationship With Government And Politics Questionnaire

As you consider all of these questions, be willing to look at your political views and the reflected views of the candidates for president. Do their words, actions, or history seem congruent? How does your relationship with a particular candidate (a relationship usually felt because you believe you are related in beliefs) fit with your answers to these questions? This is complex. We are complex people.

As you look at your history, note the following things:

1. Did you grow up in a "crazy-making" family where believed "truths," commitments, rules in the family, relationships with others, or other matters of importance often changed, with no acknowledgement of the expressed and recorded views of yesterday?
2. Did you grow up in a family belonging to a rigid, closed system of religion?
3. Did you grow up in, or later choose, a particular political party within a strong peer group?

4. Were your parents very involved in politics, or had they always belonged to a particular party?
5. Were there strongly held values in your family and with other mentors?
6. Did you feel valued in your family? Were you *valued more* if you adopted their beliefs/values?
7. Was there much anger in your family, expressed or withheld?
8. Was there much shaming in your family?
9. Have you experienced abuse for your beliefs or values? If so, was this directed at values and beliefs you adopted from your family?
10. Are you easily influenced?
11. Was there a pattern of blaming in your family, often when it was undeserved or untrue?
12. Was there prejudice in your family, with important peers, and/or other mentors? Whom and what were the prejudices about?
13. Were there denial and/or lying in your family when it best suited someone's position, including parents?
14. Does what I have written in this chapter make you angry? Has it made you more aware of yourself in any way or made you feel you might want to change anything?

CHAPTER TWENTY ONE

RELATIONSHIP WITH AGING AND END OF LIFE

The importance of a full-filled "bucket list"

By now, we are pretty completely "stewed." I believe that our relationship with aging and facing the end of life is directly related to what extent we have self-actualized and fulfilled our most important dreams. Most people settle for living out their lives in a way that greatly limits this. Self-actualization doesn't just include finding the most fulfilling career or making a lot of money. These may be part of it, but first there must be the ability or achievement of loving Self and having fulfilling relationship(s). First, I must feel good about me, and then I can add realization of some or all of my dreams to this as the icing on the cake. These goals must be mine, not my parents, or from competition with my siblings or with a mate.

Facing the end of life often includes some small illnesses or perhaps a life-threatening one, and this makes the process harder. You often find yourself in one of several doctor's offices. Again, it will be easier to manage if you are at peace with yourself and what you have achieved. You will be more likely to surrender to these conditions and the process of aging, without giving up. You will find ways to stay active and be likely to want to help others. As Erik Erikson wrote in his definition of developmental stages, a healthy end of life will include giving to others, such as grandchildren, the community, and sharing life wisdom.

People too often retire with dreams of relaxing, etc., but have had their identity so tied up with their work, have no hobbies, and have never allowed themselves to really dream and plan for staying active and involved with people in their retirement. They end up depressed.

If you grew up in a family where there was trauma around death, darkness and doom, you may carry a lot of fear about it. If you had parents who were old before they actually were old, with a negative view about aging, you may have fear.

A young relative of mine was forced as a small boy to view his father's dead body in a casket. As I and other mourners watched, he stiffened his body and had to be carried to the front of the church for the viewing. I always have remembered the terrified look on the boy's face and wondered how this has affected him, especially as he aged.

Other people have told me stories of experiencing many losses during their youth, of siblings, parents, and grandparents, in addition to young friends. The impact of these multiple losses and the ever-present grieving in the home greatly has affected them.

One woman who experienced a lot of losses says she has fearful thoughts of her death daily. I believe she was traumatized by the constant facing of death as a child. Besides many losses of close ones, she lived most of her young days expecting to find her diabetic, alcoholic mother dead. To protect herself from this fear, she often wished her mother to die, probably because going through the constant expectation was too much for a little girl to handle. Adult children often expect the worst, to prepare for what they fear, not to be surprised by it. We call it "waiting for the other shoe to drop."

Many people try to deal with their fear of death by clinging to religious beliefs, which promise life everlasting. Of course, these promises require a lot of strict rules, including only belonging to their particular sect. Since time began, man has created gods for whom they needed to behave in certain ways and do certain things for, to achieve life in the hereafter. Some religious sects, for example, require you to be baptized by their church, regardless of whether you already were baptized in another Christian church. Many more radical fundamentalists require that you interpret their Bible, Koran, or other teachings from their history literally only in the way that they do. The Islamic sects declare their interpretations and rituals as the only way. The ancient pagans had good gods and bad gods to whom they sacrificed people.

There are some who believe that they are chosen, so it doesn't matter what they do, morally or not, and that other people cannot get into this privileged group, such as the now famous C Street group in Washington D.C.. And, it goes on and on. But, all promise life everlasting, if you follow their religious beliefs and practices. Those who have experienced any of these religious sects often have had a life filled with fear of whether they will really go to heaven, or be punished forever. Besides the need of people in these groups to feel special, it is all about fear of death. These individual sects inherently say that we are not all created equal, not all entitled to or will achieve salvation.

Though there are many abusive practices at the highest levels of these various religious sects, the members tend to hang in, accustomed to "crazy making" from their families of origin, and afraid to leave.

People often think that when they are older than 60 or 70, it is too late to heal wounds from childhood. This is definitely not true. It can be incredible to experience so much reward in just a short period of time when you have more of your true Self and are not burdened with family-of-origin baggage, which affects every stage of your life. Discarding emotional baggage gives you more energy, more interest in life, and a clearer and more positive outlook. I have seen people become more physically youthful just from shedding baggage. You can learn to treasure yourself and, therefore, your final years of life. In doing so, it creates more attention toward body, mind, and spirit to stay healthy and enjoy yourself.

People often begin thinking of regrets and wishing they had taken other paths in their lives and loves. These regrets are sometimes things such as having or living with the disease of alcoholism or other drug addiction, choosing not to finish school or continue more schooling, choosing not to have children, being unable to have a career, not taking a particular dream trip. It often is not too late, but their mind-set says they are too old.

Jan shared that she regretted not having children. She got caught up in building her career and kept telling her husband they could have children later. At age 38, she had to have a hysterectomy, which ended her plans to have children. Her husband was not willing to adopt, so they lived childless. When he died at 65, leaving her at age 58 with no other family, she was devastated. She became a guardian ad-litem and a big sister. This gave her some of the connection she had missed by not having children.

Jim, turning 60, had been a hedge fund broker for many years. He was wealthy and could easily retire, but he felt unfulfilled. He regretted not having pursued his dream of being a professor of economics. When he investigated, he found that he could still teach and was welcomed not only for his appropriate education level, but also for his work experience.

Maryanne regretted that she had not chosen to travel more and even possibly live in another country, while doing something useful for others. At age 68, she applied to the Peace Corp, and was accepted. She taught for two years on an island in the West Indies.

Harry regretted that he had quit school to get married. Right away, his wife became pregnant, and it was necessary to provide for the three of them as a head of house. More children quickly followed. He wanted to go back to school but usually was working two jobs to support the family. At 50, with most of the children gone and on their own, he went back to school, persisted to a graduate degree in social work, and, began a new career.

We live in a truly frightening world. The kind of boundaries we once had no longer exist. We can easily travel into unsafe places, even in the same town or city. Fewer of us know or interact with our neighbors. We are isolated in many ways from community protection. People from different countries and walks of life intermingle, and we are unaware of who they are or what they may intend. There are wars in many places, because of differing ideas about what should be individual private beliefs, mostly about religion. For an adult child with deep fear issues, this can mean he/she will be afraid to venture out in the world to pursue goals and dreams, especially when getting older and feeling less sure of Self. If we have come from a frightening home and are fear-based, we will be more inclined to focus so much on trying to get safe, that we will be unable to expand our horizons. It does not have to be this way.

Rather than worrying so much about what comes after death, if we are healthy and less fear-based, we can focus on how we can full-fill our dreams, help others, and take healthy risks. This can make our relationship with aging more productive and rewarding, and make death and the end of life a less fearful time.

Questionnaire on Aging and End of Life

1. How did your family (parents/relatives) relate to aging and facing end of life?
2. Did you experience a lot of losses (deaths) while growing up?
3. Were there traumatic losses? Explain.
4. Are you afraid of death?
5. What are your spiritual and/or religious beliefs about death?
6. How do you feel about aging?
7. If you are older than 50, are you working to keep yourself active and healthy?
8. If you could, what would you change about your past choices?
9. Can you think of how you could still realize a lost dream?

Chapter Twenty Two

HEALING OUR EMOTIONAL WOUNDS

Are achieving better relationships worth striving to find my true Self?

Healing our emotional wounds, therefore becoming available for healthy relationships, may look like an awesome challenge. I won't kid you that it can be done quickly. Time required is relative to three things:

1) How old and how deep are some of your wounds?
2) How much healing do you want?
3) How much are you willing to invest in time and cost?

These are not decisions that you need to make up front. You probably don't know the depth of your emotional wounds, until you have explored that. You may decide at any point that you have reached a place in healing that is sufficient for you or that you may come back to it at a later date. How much you are willing to spend in time and cost is also a decision most people make as they proceed in efforts toward recovery.

Many of you may be familiar with twelve-step programs. They certainly are loaded in attendance by adult children. All of the programs are about healing addictions, the "using," and the "thinking," so whoever is in these programs carry emotional wounds. These programs are primarily a place to stop the addictive process, to achieve abstinence from a particular addiction disease. However, they also offer much to the emotionally wounded through working on the twelve steps, and helping members learn to reconnect with others. They offer a lot of support and empathy, and provide sponsors who coach them on how to change their lives for sobriety. They do not, and are not meant to go to the roots of emotional wounds, where much deeper healing can occur. These emotional wounds are underneath every addictive process and are lurking to be triggered and create relapse, or other dysfunctional behaviors. Whether you see yourself as having an addiction (see Chapter 15 on addictions) or not, you can very much benefit from a twelve-step program such as Al-Anon, which is for people who are addicted to other people, or have someone addicted (or who displays the symptoms of addiction), who is important in their life, in many cases to an addict. There is also ACOA, Adult Children of Alcoholics, which speaks to anyone from a dysfunctional family. My belief is that if everyone worked the twelve steps, there would be no war.

Many of my clients have read many self-help books, listened to how-to tapes, taken "A Course in Miracles," and tried various new age techniques, or similar things. These tools can be very helpful to motivate you to believe there can be change and sometimes to make some minor changes. However, without psychotherapy along with them, most of their benefits will disappear in a fairly short time, just as happens with diets. You will be stuck in many cases with, "I know what is wrong and why but can't seem to just change!"

There is also behavioral therapy and cognitive therapy, which also offer benefits in helping one change and to even understand why you do what you do. My experience has been, personally and as a therapist, that these alone do not motivate real deep and lasting change, because they do not focus on our emotions and the deeper healing of these wounds, for the most part.

My recommendation is to find a therapist who does experiential therapy. These include such techniques as gestalt work, inner child work, psychodrama, a combination of psychodrama with other experiential (action) methods, such as family sculpting. The important idea is to participate in action therapy, not just talk therapy. In my opinion, a good therapist is an eclectic therapist, using a combination of some of the above with behavioral and cognitive. The important thing is that experiential methods will access emotions. Adult children require emotional surgery to heal. Finally, I believe, and studies show, that group therapy is the most effective way to promote growth and change, and takes less time than individual talk therapy alone.

Your therapist's job is to help you find your true Self. If you feel lost, you will want to explore your goals and dreams. You may think there are none but will find, with the right therapist, that there is a little child in you, who knows the answers to this. There are no rules about what one's goals and/or dreams should be, because they are uniquely yours. Whatever you end up achieving should answer to you and not be looked back upon as "if only I had followed my own dreams." At just about any age, it is not too late to free yourself from whatever controls keep you from moving toward a dream. People find amazing ways to do this when determined. There can be many variations of how you realize your dream(s), not just seen from one angle.

I suggest you start by answering the questions I have written at the end of each chapter. Really think about them and write down all you know. Then, if you are willing and want to change your ability to form fulfilling relationships, find a therapist who has done their own therapy (very, very important), has good training (not just an education degree), and specializes in family-of-origin therapy. And, again, consider finding a twelve-step program that speaks to you. Good luck!

QUESTIONNAIRE ON HEALING SELF

1. Write a history of your life, with emphasis on special and traumatic or very painful events, starting in your childhood.
2. Write a list of your regrets of things done or not done, as well as choices you did or did not make, which you feel were important turning points in your life.
3. What do you wish you could do about those choices now? Can you?
4. In what areas have you had trouble with relationships?
5. Have you ever explored your history and emotional wounds in therapy?
6. Do you sometimes not know how to define who you really are?

Questions?

Did you find this book helpful? Do you have a better understanding of how we are so much of who we come from? If you have comments or questions, please visit me on my website at:

http://centerforselfdiscovery.net/

ACKNOWLEDGEMENTS

First, I want to acknowledge my cheerleader, Deni B. Sher, who pushed me to begin again and continue my writing after a four-year hiatus, because of illness. She also worked with me on the first editing of my book, which also kept me moving.

There were many others who encouraged me, asking when my book would be done. These were my friend and colleague Marlys Freeman, my therapy group members, (and all of my group members over thirty years who have taught me so much), my friend, Jack Bloomfield, my friend Mary Lill Lee, and my childhood friend, Ann Crytser. Some of them read parts of my book and gave me feedback.

I will always be grateful to my mentors, who taught me so much about doing experiential work and family-of-origin therapy: Virginia Satir, John Heider, Glory King, Sharon W. Cruse, Nina Garcia, and Dale Buchanan.

Joyce Sweeny was very helpful and knowledgeable as my editor, being very kind in her critiques.

For my sister, I am always grateful for her interest and willingness to work with me on our relationship, which was so badly wounded in our childhood. She is always there for me today.

I am forever grateful to my partner, Carey Elizabeth Matthews, for what I have learned from her in our life and work together, and for her support and patience with my endeavor to write this book.

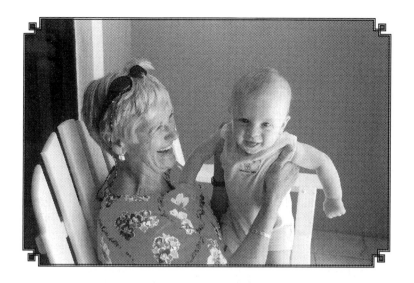

ABOUT THE AUTHOR

Anne Salter is in private practice in Delray Beach, Florida, working with couples, adults, the elderly, and families, individually and in on-going groups. Her focus is on healing family relationships that influence all relationships, advanced-level recovery, and trauma work.

Anne can be reached by phone at: 561-736-0793; by e-mail: centerforselfdiscovery@comcast.net.